REASONING AND SENSE-MAKING
Problems and Activities
for Grades 5–8

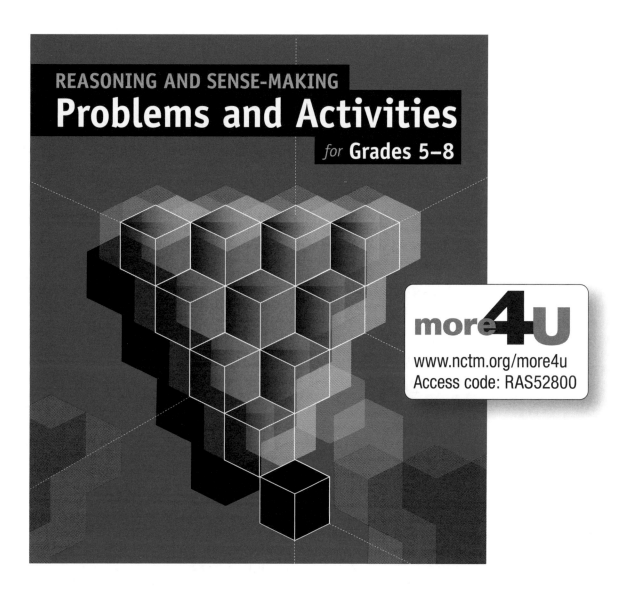

REASONING AND SENSE-MAKING
Problems and Activities
for Grades 5–8

more**4u**
www.nctm.org/more4u
Access code: RAS52800

Elizabeth D. Phillips
Editor
Michigan State University, East Lansing, Michigan

Judith S. Zawojewski
Editor
Illinois Institute of Technology, Chicago, Illinois

NATIONAL COUNCIL OF
TEACHERS OF MATHEMATICS

Library of Congress Cataloging-in-Publication Data

Reasoning and sense-making problems and activities for grades 5-8 /
Elizabeth D. Phillips, Judith Zawojewski, editor[s].
    p. cm.
 ISBN 978-0-87353-632-5
 1. Problem solving--Study and teaching (Middle school)--Activity
programs. 2. Mathematics--Study and teaching (Middle school)--Activity
programs. I. Phillips, Elizabeth Difanis, 1937- II. Zawojewski, Judith.
III. National Council of Teachers of Mathematics.
 QA63.R37 2011
 372.7--dc23
                              2011021047

The National Council of Teachers of Mathematics is a public voice
of mathematics education, supporting teachers to ensure equitable mathematics
learning of the highest quality for all students through vision, leadership, professional
development, and research.

Printed in the United States of America

Contents

INTRODUCTION 1

CHAPTER 1: NUMBER AND OPERATIONS 5

  Ordering, Comparing, and Equivalence 5

    Problem 1: Customers Cut the Cake 6

    Problem 2: Identifying Fractions Near 0, 1/2, and 1 8

    Problem 3: Exploring Numerators and Denominators 10

    Problem 4: Here's Looking at Percents 12

  Operations on Rational Numbers 15

    Problem 5: Multiplication by Decimals Near 0, 1/2, and 1 15

    Problem 6: Operations on a Fraction Number Line 18

    Problem 7: Patterns with Fractions 20

  Proportions 23

    Problem 8: Exploring the Size of a Million Dollars 23

    Problem 9: Capture Recapture 24

  Exponents 26

    Problem 10: Patterns in the Powers Chart 26

CHAPTER 2: MEASUREMENT AND GEOMETRY 31

  Part 1: Measurement 31

  Introducing Measurement 32

    Problem 1: Creating Metric ID Cards 32

    Problem 2: How Big Is Your Foot? 34

  Measuring Circles 36

    Problem 3: Circumference of a Circle 36

    Problem 4: Area of Circles 38

    Problem 5: Grazing Cows 41

  Measuring Polygons 43

    Problem 6: Areas of Polygons 43

    Problem 7: Area of Squares and Square Roots 45

    Problem 8: Finding Lengths of Line Segments 48

    Problem 9: Squares and the Pythagorean Theorem 51

    Problem 10: Proving the Pythagorean Theorem 54

Problem 11: Using the Pythagorean Theorem.. 56

Measuring Surface Area and Volume **57**

Problem 12: Surface Area 57

Problem 13: Volume 60

Similar Figures **63**

Problem 14: Similar Shapes 63

Problem 15: Building Staircases 66

Part 2: Visualizing and Representing Shapes **68**

Problem 16: Exploring Cubes 68

Problem 17: Representing Buildings Made from Cubes 72

Problem 18: Parallelogram and Triangular Grids 75

Problem 19: Slides, Flips, and Turns 77

CHAPTER 3: DATA AND CHANCE.. **83**

Problem 1: Is This Game Fair?.. 84

Problem 2: Monte Carlo Simulation 87

Problem 3: A Look at Average Wage 90

Problem 4: Light-Bulb Life 93

Problem 5: Family Combinations of Boys and Girls 96

Problem 6: Montana Red Dog 98

CHAPTER 4: PATTERNS AND FUNCTIONS.. **103**

Problem 1: The Race—Linear Functions.. 103

Problem 2: Rumors—Exponential Functions 107

Problem 3: Folding Paper—Exponential Functions....................................... 110

Problem 4: Miracle Mike—Linear and Exponential Functions 114

Problem 5: Cube Coloring—Linear, Quadratic, and Cubic Functions.......... 117

Problem 6: Maximum Area—Quadratic Functions....................................... 120

Problem 7: Reading Graphs 126

Problem 8: Bottle Functions—an Experiment 130

Problem 9: The Function Machine.. 134

APPENDIX A: Chapter 2 Blackline Masters... **139**

Blackline Master 2.1: Square-Dot Paper.. 140

Blackline Master 2.2: Five-by-Five Dot Grids 141

Blackline Master 2.3: Centimeter Grid Paper 142

Blackline Master 2.4: Isometric Dot Paper 143

Blackline Master 2.5: Grazing Cows 144

Blackline Master 2.6: The Area of Polygons 145

Blackline Master 2.7: Proving the Pythagorean Theorem 146

Blackline Master 2.8: Similar Shapes 147

Blackline Master 2.9: Building Staircases 149

Blackline Master 2.10: Representing Buildings Made from Cubes 151

Blackline Master 2.11: Parallelogram and Triangular Grids 153

Blackline Master 2.12: Slides, Flips, and Turns 154

APPENDIX B: Chapter 3 Blackline Masters **157**

Blackline Master 3.1: Sum of Seven: A Two-Person Game 158

Blackline Master 3.2: Sum of Seven Recording Sheet 159

Blackline Master 3.3: A Look at Average Wage 160

Blackline Master 3.4: Light-Bulb Life 162

Blackline Master 3.5: Montana Red Dog Recording Sheet 163

Introduction

IN **MARCH** 1989, the National Council of Teachers of Mathematics officially released *Curriculum and Evaluation Standards for School Mathematics* (NCTM 1989). The document provided a vision and a framework for strengthening the mathematics curriculum in kindergarten through grade 12 in North American schools. During NCTM's development of the document, it became apparent that the document would need a plethora of examples to illustrate how to implement the vision in the grades K–12 classroom. This, in turn, led to NCTM inviting leaders in the mathematics education community to write a series of supplementary books for teachers. The purpose of those books, referred to as the Addenda series, was to support the implementation of the 1989 *Standards* document. Although NCTM has produced a number of documents since then (e.g., *Principles and Standards for School Mathematics* [2000]; *Curriculum Focal Points for Prekindergarten through Grade 8 Mathematics: A Quest for Coherence* [2006]), each one builds on and refines the original vision set forth in *Curriculum and Evaluation Standards*. Therefore, much of the content in the Addenda series applies as extensively today as it did the 1990s. In this spirit, NCTM's Educational Materials Committee invited us, Elizabeth Phillips and Judith Zawojewski, in 2006 to coordinate developing this book as a collection of the best of the Addenda series, grades 5–8.

The problems selected for this book represent important content for today's middle school mathematics curriculum. We chose them because they emphasize the roles of representation, generalization, problem solving, and connections in mathematics learning and teaching. These four practices first put forth by NCTM (2000) also appear in the set of Mathematical Practices that the Common Core State Standards for Mathematics (CCSSM) described in 2010. The eight Mathematical Practices are as follows:

1. Make sense of problems and persevere in solving them;

2. Reason abstractly and quantitatively;

3. Construct viable arguments and critique the reasoning of others;

4. Model with mathematics;

5. Use appropriate tools strategically;

6. Attend to precision;

7. Look for and make sense of structure; and

8. Look for and express regularity in repeated reasoning.

We do not intend the resulting set of problems to be comprehensive, because complete coverage is not possible in a book of this size. Therefore, we left many worthy problems and activities behind, as opportunities for the reader to revisit some of the experiences from the original series. Further, the introduction to each of the series' original books is a rich source of information on that book's mathematics content. We believe that all the original books would be well worth a reread.

We have organized this book into four chapters: Number and Operations, Measurement and Geometry, Data and Chance, and Algebra. The chapters draw on a variety of problems that the Addenda series, Grades 5–8—*Developing Number Sense in the Middle Grades; Understanding Rational Numbers and Proportions; Measurement in the Middle Grades; Geometry in the Middle Grades; Dealing with Data and Chance;* and *Patterns and Functions*—originally published. We have placed some of the problems that occurred in a given chapter in the Addenda in different chapters. For example, problem 10 in chapter 1, Number and Operations, originally occurred in the *Patterns and Functions* book. To present all the various problems and activities in one publication, we adapted the original work to fit a common format and provide consistent support for implementing the activities. Therefore, although we have noted each problem's origin, we adapted, added to, and subtracted from the original work to create a cohesive set of experiences for this book. We composed each problem with a goal statement, a list of the needed materials, possible solutions, teacher's notes, and ideas for extensions. The teacher's notes include the problem's mathematical goals, essential information for implementing the problem, elaboration on students' possible strategies, sample questions for use in class discussion, and commentary on and answers to the questions. Throughout the book we have identified some situations that represent the CCSSM Mathematical Practices. Since all the problems and activities in this book reflect the Mathematical Practice, "Make sense of problems and persevere in solving them," we have not always listed this practice. We invite the reader to look for more instances of the Mathematical Practices and to add more questions, explanation, organization, and pedagogy to adapt the experiences to each unique classroom setting.

We hope that you find this rich collection of activities a valuable resource as it supplements your curriculum, and that it helps you, together with your students, develop deeper understandings of, and appreciation for, the important ideas in middle school mathematics.

REFERENCES

Bezuk, Nadine. "From the File: Easy Pieces." *Arithmetic Teacher* 36 (February 1989): 3.

Curcio, Frances J., Nadine S. Bezuk, Barbara E. Armstrong, Alice F. Artzt, Heidi Janzen, Steven T. Klass, Tami Martin, J. Lewis McNeece, Claire M. Newman, Francine Sicklick, Susan B. Turkel, and Judith S. Zawojewski. *Understanding Rational Numbers and Proportions.* Reston, Va.: National Council of Teachers of Mathematics, 1994.

Geddes, Dorothy, Julianna Bove, Irene Fortunato, David J. Fuys, Jessica Morgenstern, and Rosamond Welchman-Tischler. *Geometry in the Middle Grades.* Reston, Va.: National Council of Teachers of Mathematics, 1992.

Geddes, Dorothy, Robert Berkman, Iris Fearon, Michael Fishenfeld, Caroline Forlano, David J. Fuys, Jodi Goldstein, and Rosamond Welchman. *Measurement in the Middle Grades.* Reston, Va.: National Council of Teachers of Mathematics, 1994.

National Council of Teachers of Mathematics (NCTM). *Curriculum and Evaluation Standards for School Mathematics.* Reston, Va.: NCTM, 1989.

———. *Principles and Standards for School Mathematics.* Reston, Va.: NCTM, 2000.

———. *Curriculum Focal Points for Prekindergarten through Grade 8 Mathematics: A Quest for Coherence.* Reston, Va.: NCTM, 2006.

Phillips, Elizabeth, Theodore Gardella, Constance Kelly, and Jacqueline Stewart. *Patterns and Functions.* Reston, Va.: National Council of Teachers of Mathematics, 1991.

Reys, Barbara J., Rita Barger, Maxim Bruckheimer, Barbara Dougherty, Jack Hope, Linda Menbke, Zvia Markovits, Andy Parnas, Sue Reehm, Ruthi Sturdevant, and Marianne Weber. *Developing Number Sense in the Middle Grades.* Reston, Va.: National Council of Teachers of Mathematics, 1992.

Zawojewski, Judith S., Gary Brooks, Lynn Dinkelkamp, Eunice D. Goldberg, Howard Goldberg, Arthur Hyde, Tess Jackson, Marsha Landau, Hope Martin, Jeri Nowakowski, Sandy Paull, Albert P. Shulte, Philip Wagreich, and Barbara Wilmot. *Dealing with Data and Chance.* Reston, Va.: National Council of Teachers of Mathematics, 1991.

Number and Operations

WE HAVE selected this chapter's problems from three books in NCTM's
Addenda series, Grades 5–8: *Developing Number Sense, Understanding
Rational Numbers and Proportions,* and *Patterns and Functions.* This chapter
has four sections: (1) ordering, comparing, and equivalence; (2) operations on
rational numbers; (3) applications of proportions; and (4) exponents. We do not
intend that this set represent comprehensive coverage of the topics, but instead
that it emphasize deep conceptual development, problem solving, reasoning,
and connections across the curricular topics, and that it link previously learned
concepts and skills with more advanced knowledge and applications. (Note that
chapter 2, Measurement and Geometry, introduces irrational numbers.)

The Addenda series addressed number and operations largely through developing number sense and operations sense. "Number sense is not a finite entity
that a student either has or does not have, nor it is a unit that can be 'taught'
and then put aside" (Reys et al. 1992, pp. 3–4). Instead, number and operations
sense *develops* hand-in-hand with deep conceptual understanding when students
engage in sustained, challenging sense making and problem solving. The selected
problems emphasize problem solving, reasoning, and connections. The goal is
to include examples of problems that can help students develop intuitions about
number relationships and operations across the full set of rational numbers.
Teacher's notes that show how one can adapt the problem to one's own environment, and that offer ideas for extending the problem to further lessons and units,
accompany each of the problems.

Ordering, Comparing, and Equivalence

Foundational to rational-number concepts are the notions of ordering, comparing, and equivalence. Conceptualizing the relative size of numbers requires
attention to the size of the unit and the number of equivalent parts in the unit
or in groupings of the unit. Visualizing and using various representations (e.g.,
regions, number lines, fractions, decimals, percents) help develop one's ability to
compare and order numbers intuitively and powerfully. The Customers Cut the
Cake problem requires students to analyze and visualize creating fractional parts
while solving a complex problem. Identifying Fractions Near 0, $\frac{1}{2}$, and 1 emphasizes estimation with fractions as a precursor to estimating operations. Exploring Numerators and Denominators analyzes the general relationships between
numerators and denominators with respect to the relative size of fractions. Here's
Looking at Percents has students make connections among various representations of percents.

Common Core Mathematical Practices
All the activities in this chapter provide opportunities for students to *reason abstractly and quantitatively.*

Problem 1: Customers Cut the Cake

(Adapted from *Understanding Rational Numbers and Proportions,* activity 1, pp. 13–15; activity 2, p. 15, by Nadine S. Bezuk, Barbara E. Armstrong, Heidi Janzen, and Steven T. Klass [Curcio et al. 1994])

Each day Benny makes several rectangular sheet cakes, which he cuts into eighths. He sells $1/_8$ of a sheet cake for $1.59. As part of a new promotional campaign for his store, he wants to cut his sheet cakes into eighths in a different way each day. Each day, the customer whose suggestion Benny uses to cut the cakes into eighths wins a free piece of cake.

- What restrictions must be put on the pieces cut from the cake?

- What are some of the different ways to cut the cake?

- Prepare a presentation that verifies that your cake cuts are equivalent parts.

Solutions to Problem 1

Customers Cut the Cake

Restrictions: Each piece must contain the same amount of cake to make the size of the piece sold for $1.59 consistent for all customers.

Different ways to cut the cake: Answers will vary, but examples include the following:

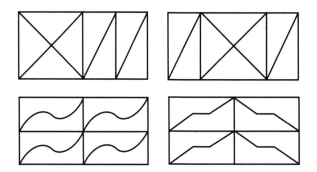

Verification: One way to verify that a solution does in fact result in eighths is to cut up a rectangular piece of paper representing the cake into individual eighths, and then check the area equivalence of each piece by placing one over the other to determine that each piece exactly covers the other—using dissection (i.e., further cutting) of one of the pieces as needed.

Teacher's Notes

This problem's purpose is to explore equivalence in fractional parts when the shapes of the pieces are different. The problem challenges students to dissect regions of the whole—the rectangular sheet cake—to form equivalent areas in different ways. To do so, they can sketch their ideas on paper or use rectangular sheets of paper to model the cakes. Some students may have a limited view and think that all the cuts must be parallel to one side of the rectangle. Have different students share their various initial ideas after a few minutes to help some students break out of their "parallel to sides" thinking. Near the end of class, ask students to post their different ideas on the walls around the classroom. As students have time during this and other class periods, have them agree or disagree with each displayed cake cutting by attaching their initialed agree-or-disagree decision to that display on a sticky note. Require those who disagree to use a larger sticky note, so they can include an explanation of why they disagree. After two days, have a whole-class discussion about those proposed cake cuts for which students have not agreed on the equivalence of the resulting pieces of cake.

The notion of equivalence in this problem goes beyond conventionally taught computation rules, establishing equivalence between two fractions by reasoning about the geometry—considering relationships among various dimensions—or by dissecting regions. Note that students do not necessarily have to accomplish cake cuts with straight lines, as illustrated in the solution. The reasoning needed to establish the equivalence of shapes formed by curved lines can be very challenging, but you can implement an intuitive approach by having students cut the shapes apart physically and arrange the resulting shapes manually to show the equivalence in area.

Common Core Mathematical Practices
When students pose their ideas, and critique those of others, the situation encourages them to *construct viable arguments and critique the reasoning of others.*

Extensions

- Imagine that Benny is conducting a second contest, this time for his employees. As part of a new promotional campaign for this store, each day he wants to feature sheet cakes cut into four pieces in a different way. The pieces do *not* have to be equivalent in size for this promotion. Benny has challenged his employees to suggest interesting ways to cut the cake into four pieces and determine each piece's fair, new price. (Benny normally sells $1/_8$ of a sheet cake for $1.59.) What are some of the different ways to cut the cakes, and how much should each piece cost?

- Given that $1/_8$ of a sheet cake costs $1.59 and a whole cake costs $12.72, have students create tables that show the cost for different fractional parts of the cake. For example, students can complete the following table:

Size of Piece of Cake	Cost
$\dfrac{1}{3}$	
$\dfrac{2}{3}$	
$\dfrac{3}{3}$	

Problem 2: Identifying Fractions Near 0, ¹/₂, and 1

(Adapted from *Developing Number Sense*, activity 18, p. 30 [Reys et al. 1992]; original source Bezuk [1989])

- Sort the following fractions into three groups—those close to 0, to $^1/_2$, and to 1.

$$\frac{4}{7} \quad \frac{1}{7} \quad \frac{8}{9} \quad \frac{4}{9} \quad \frac{12}{11} \quad \frac{6}{11} \quad \frac{5}{12}$$

$$\frac{2}{12} \quad \frac{41}{48} \quad \frac{41}{78} \quad \frac{6}{151} \quad \frac{79}{151} \quad \frac{299}{595} \quad \frac{19}{595}$$

- Describe how you thought about making the sorting decision for each fraction.

- Write a general rule that will help someone *always* identify fractions close to 0, to $^1/_2$, and to 1.

Solution to Problem 2

Close to 0: $\dfrac{1}{7}, \dfrac{2}{12}, \dfrac{6}{151}, \dfrac{19}{595}$

Close to $\dfrac{1}{2}$: $\dfrac{4}{7}, \dfrac{4}{9}, \dfrac{6}{11}, \dfrac{5}{12}, \dfrac{41}{78}, \dfrac{79}{151}, \dfrac{299}{595}$

Close to 1: $\dfrac{8}{9}, \dfrac{12}{11}, \dfrac{41}{48}$

Close to 0: the numerator is very small compared to the denominator.

Close to $\dfrac{1}{2}$: the denominator is about twice the size of the numerator.

Close to 1: the numerator is very close in value to the denominator.

Teacher's Notes

Identifying fractions close to 0, to $\frac{1}{2}$, and to 1 assumes that students have a sound understanding of the meaning of fractions as parts of wholes (e.g., in regions and number-line models). Before students try this problem, they should be able to imagine mentally an approximate region filled in for any given fraction. If students do not have mental images handy, the teacher can draw a series of circles on the chalkboard and have different students shade in an amount that approximates each fraction in the list. As they do so, have them explain their thinking. These explanations are likely to reveal that many students already use 0, $\frac{1}{2}$, and 1 as benchmarks when trying to estimate a fraction's size. Repeat this step with rectangular regions of the same shape and size. Similarly, you should use a number-line model to review the meaning of each fraction in the problem.

The goal in this problem is for students to translate their conceptual and visual knowledge of fractions into generalized regularities concerning the relationship between the sizes of the numerators and denominators. By the end of the problem, students construct their own general rules for deciding whether a fraction is close to 0, $\frac{1}{2}$, or 1.

Extensions

- After students shade in circles to represent the approximate amount for each fraction above, draw a very long line segment on the chalkboard. Label the ends 0 and 1, and place $\frac{1}{2}$ in the middle. Have volunteers come to the board to indicate approximately where each fraction will be on the number line, and mark the location once the class confirms the placement. Extend this activity by erasing the line segment, drawing it again, and labeling the ends 0 and 2. Repeat the same process, but use these different reference points for what constitutes the whole unit.

- Have students translate their verbal descriptions of general rules for deciding how to sort fractions as being close to 0, $\frac{1}{2}$, and 1 into rules that use variables. For example, they could state the rule for deciding "close to $\frac{1}{2}$" in the solution box above as follows:

Given a fraction $\frac{a}{b}$, a is approximately $\frac{1}{2}$ b (or b is approximately 2a).

Solution to Extensions for Problem 2

Generalizing rules for fractions close to 0 or 1 into variables is more challenging than generalizing the rule for close to $\frac{1}{2}$. For example, *a fraction close to 1 would be one in which the difference between the numerator (a) and denominator (b) is less than x percent of b, where x must be less than 25.*

Problem 3: Exploring Numerators and Denominators

(Adapted from *Developing Number Sense*, activity 22, p. 33 [Reys et al. 1992])

- Suppose that *a*, *b*, and *c* each represents a whole number different from 0. Also suppose that $a > b > c$. What can you say about how each of these fractions relates to 1?

$$\frac{a}{b} \qquad \frac{b}{a} \qquad \frac{b}{c}$$

$$\frac{c}{b} \qquad \frac{a}{c} \qquad \frac{c}{a}$$

- If possible, tell which in each pair is larger. Justify your decision.

$$\frac{a}{c} \text{ or } \frac{b}{c} \qquad \frac{a}{b} \text{ or } \frac{b}{b} \qquad \frac{a}{b} \text{ or } \frac{a}{c}$$

Solution to Problem 3

$\frac{a}{b} > 1, \quad \frac{b}{a} < 1, \quad \frac{b}{c} > 1, \quad \frac{c}{b} < 1, \quad \frac{a}{c} > 1, \quad \frac{c}{a} < 1$

$\frac{a}{c} > \frac{b}{c}$: Since both fractions involve a whole unit cut into "*c*" parts, then the fraction with the most parts would be larger. Since $a > b$, then $\frac{a}{c} > \frac{b}{c}$.

$\frac{a}{b} > \frac{b}{b}$: Since both fractions involve a whole unit cut into "*b*" parts, then the fraction with the most parts would be larger. Since $a > b$, then $\frac{a}{b} > \frac{b}{b}$. (Also, since $\frac{b}{b} = 1$, then $\frac{a}{b} > 1$.)

$\frac{a}{b} < \frac{a}{c}$: Since the whole unit in the first fraction is cut into "*b*" parts and the whole unit in the second fraction is cut into "*c*" parts, and $c < b$, then the parts in the second fraction are larger than the parts in the first fraction. Thus, $\frac{a}{b} < \frac{a}{c}$.

Teacher's Notes

The first part of this problem has students make generalizations about fractions by comparing the numerator and denominator. To get students started, the teacher can have them consider specific values, for example, $a = 3$, $b = 2$, and $c = 1$. When students make the specific comparisons, they will need to think about how the two values in the fraction form one entity. Then, assign different values to a, b, and c. After trying a few different values for the variables to generalize, students will be in a position to consider how the values represented by the general characteristics of the numerator and denominator influence the value of the fraction. For example, students considering $^a/_b$ where $a > b$, need to generate the idea that in every instance, the general fraction will represent a quantity greater than 1.

In the problem's second part, students will compare two generalized fractions. For example, when students consider whether $^a/_b$ is larger than $^a/_c$ they may think about the relative size of the parts of the whole unit to make the comparison. In this example, because $b > c$, and because the assumption is that the size of the whole unit is constant, then the parts of a whole unit cut up into c pieces will each be bigger than the parts of a whole unit cut up into b pieces (i.e., the denominators). Since the same number of parts are involved in each fraction (i.e., the numerators), then $^a/_c > ^a/_b$.

Although the focus of this problem is on the relative size of the fractions, the problem is embedded in the use of variables, providing a good opportunity for students to work with variables that really are *variable*. In conventional prealgebra work, students often evaluate expressions by substituting specific values for a variable and solving the resulting equations to find out what specific number the variable represents. In other words, students do not typically see a variable as truly varying, whereas this problem substantively addresses the notion of variable as varying.

Problem 4: Here's Looking at Percents

(Adapted from *Understanding Rational Numbers and Proportions,* activities 4 and 6, pp. 9, 11, and 12, by Judith S. Zawojewski [Curcio et al. 1994])

1. Obtain three large, paper unit squares (equivalent), each divided up into 10 rows of 10, or 100, smaller, equal square regions. Use a scissors to cut around each of the whole-unit squares (10 rows of 10), leaving the "hundredths" of the whole unit intact.

Common Core Mathematical Practices
When students derive patterns from abstract representations of fraction relationships, they *look for and make use of structure.*

2. Fold one of the paper unit squares, with hundredths indicated on it, along one of the center lines to form two equivalent, rectangular halves. Shade one of the halves.

   a. What are three fraction names for the amount shaded? How have you represented these fractions on the unit square?

   b. What are two decimal names for the amount shaded? How have you represented these decimals on the paper unit square?

   c. What is the percent name for the amount shaded? How have you represented this percent on the paper unit square?

Solutions to Problem 4, Question 2

(Explanations will vary.)

2a. $\frac{50}{100}$ (fifty out of one hundred squares are shaded); $\frac{5}{10}$ (five out of ten rows are shaded); $\frac{1}{2}$ (one of the two sides on either side of the fold is shaded)

2b. 0.50 (fifty hundredths is shaded), 0.5 (five of the tenths are shaded, the tenths being the columns of ten squares)

2c. 50 percent (fifty out of one hundred squares are shaded)

3. Fold the unit square used in question 2 above in half once again to form a square.

   a. What is the fraction name for each newly formed region? What is the fraction name for three of the newly formed regions?

   b. What is the decimal name for each newly formed region? What is the decimal name for three of the newly formed regions?

   c. What is the percent name for the newly formed region? What is the percent name for three of the newly formed regions?

Solutions to Problem 4, Question 3

3a. $\frac{1}{4}, \frac{3}{4}$; 3b. 0.25, 0.75; 3c. 25 percent, 75 percent

4. Fold a new paper unit square, with hundredths indicated on it, along one of its main diagonals. Shawna says that each triangular piece on either side of the fold contains 50 percent of the area of the original paper unit square. Alex disagrees, saying that the pieces are not *exactly* 50 percent. Who is correct? Why?

5. Fold the third paper unit square, with hundredths indicated on it, into thirds, forming three equivalent, rectangular parts. Analyze each third, and figure out how many of the small squares are contained in each third. Explain the precise number of hundredth squares in each third, and state the percent name. Repeat for two-thirds of the unit square.

Solutions to Problem 4, Question 4

Assuming the square is folded precisely along the diagonal, Shawna is correct, because when the square is cut along the diagonal, each half has 9 + 8 + 7 + 6 + 5 + 4 + 3 + 2 + 1 whole squares, or 45 whole squares. Along the diagonal are 10 squares that are each cut in half, so each triangle contains 10 half-squares, which is equivalent to 5 whole squares, making a total of 45 + 5, or 50, out of 100 squares in each half: 50 percent.

Solutions to Problem 4, Question 5

(Answers will vary.)

Each of the two outer rectangles has 3 rows of 10 full squares, or 30 squares in all. Each one also has a row of 10 one-third squares, which are equivalent to $3\frac{1}{3}$ additional whole squares: 30 full squares and the $3\frac{1}{3}$ additional squares indicates $33\frac{1}{3}$ percent. The middle rectangular piece has only 2 full rows of 10 squares, making 20 full squares. The middle piece also has a row of 10 two-third squares on one side and a row of 10 two-third squares on the other side, making 20 additional two-third squares. The 20 two-third squares is equivalent to $13\frac{1}{3}$ full squares, making a total of $20 + 13\frac{1}{3}$ full squares, or $33\frac{1}{3}$ percent. Thus $\frac{1}{3}$ is equivalent to $33\frac{1}{3}$ percent, and $\frac{2}{3}$ is equivalent to $66\frac{2}{3}$ percent.

Materials

☑ Three copies of a paper 10-centimeter-by-10-centimeter grid for each student, with the outline of the grid shown in bold to represent the whole unit

☑ Scissors

Teacher's Notes

This problem aims to have students explore equivalence among fractions, decimals, and percents using a concrete region, or area, model of a one whole unit divided into hundredths. The work requires that students understand the concept of tenths and hundredths as regions or parts of a whole. Students can do the first three problems individually, because after folding the whole unit squares, counting the number of hundredths squares is easy to do. That counting also offers a good opportunity to review the meaning of percent as some number out of a hundred. The last two problems, however, require that students analyze resulting partial regions (i.e., halves and thirds of a hundredth) to find an exact total number of hundredths. Students should do this step in pairs, so they can share their ideas for conducting the analysis. Conduct a class discussion in which different pairs of students describe how they figured out the exact size of the partial squares and how they combined them to form full squares.

Extensions

- Fold a whole paper unit square that is divided into hundredths (10 by 10) into eighths, then another into fifths, and another into twentieths, For each result, figure out the percent and decimal equivalents for the fraction that the region resulting from the fold represents (i.e., eighths, fifths, and twentieths).

- Begin with a paper unit square partitioned into tenths, and fold it into various fractional parts. Analyze each result to determine the percent and decimal equivalents for the fraction that the region resulting from the fold represents.

Operations on Rational Numbers

This section's problems require students to go far beyond memorized rules for computation. Computational estimation in the problem Multiplication by Decimals Near 0, $^1/_2$, and 1 draws on both a deep understanding of multiplication and a sound concept for the meanings of the numbers themselves. The problem Operations on a Fraction Number Line emphasizes the need to understand

---

Common Core Mathematical Practices

When students describe how they reason about the partial regions, they must **attend to precision** in their language and demonstration in order to communicate their reasoning clearly to their classmates.

how operations with rational numbers play out in different representational modes—in this instance, on a number line. Patterns with Fractions has students "solve problems; develop understandings of important mathematical concepts and relationships; investigate the relationships among quantities … in a pattern; generalize patterns using words or variables; extend and connect patterns; [and] construct understandings of function" (Phillips et al. 1991, p. 1).

Problem 5: Multiplication by Decimals Near 0, $^1/_2$, and 1

(Adapted from *Developing Number Sense*, activity 34, p. 40 [Reys et al. 1992])

What happens when you multiply by decimals close to 0, $^1/_2$, and 1? Explore this question by completing the table below.

	A Multiply by:		B Multiply by:		C Multiply by:	
Pick a Whole Number	0.05	0.1	0.48	0.51	0.98	1.07

1. Fill in the blanks below with 0, $^1/_2$, or 1:

   a. The multipliers in A are closest to _____.

   b. The multipliers in B are closest to _____.

   c. The multipliers in C are closest to _____.

2. Answer the following questions:

   a. In general, what happens when you multiply a whole number by decimal close to 0?

   b. In general, what happens when you multiply a whole number by a decimal close to $^1/_2$?

   c. In general, what happens when you multiply a whole number by a decimal close to 1?

Solutions to Problem 5, Questions 1 and 2

(Answers will vary but will be similar to those below.)

    1a. Column A: Close to 0

    1b. Column B: Close to $\frac{1}{2}$

    1c. Column C: Close to 1

    2a. Close to 0: The product is relatively small, closer to zero than it is to half the value of the other factor.

    2b. Close to $\frac{1}{2}$: The product is approximately half the other factor.

    2c. Close to 1: The product is close to the other factor.

Common Core Mathematical Practices

When students make generalizations about repeated calculations they **reason abstractly and quantitatively.**

3. Using what you have learned about multiplying by decimals close to 0, $^1/_2$, and 1, estimate the product for each of the following. Explain your thinking for each one, as illustrated in the first example:

- 19.76 × 0.47 is about   _____10_____ .

    (Think about the first factor—close to 20, and the second factor—close to $^1/_2$. To estimate the product, you can use 20 × $^1/_2$, which has a product of 10, so the estimate is about 10.)

- 1.09 × 27.8 is about _____.

- 0.55 × 101.67 is about _____.

- 39.8 x 0.012 is about _____.

- 0.722 × 0.99 is about _____.

Solutions to Problem 5, Question 3

(Answers may vary within 10 percent of the given estimate): about 30, about 50, about 39, about 0.7)

Materials

☑ Students may use calculators to fill out the table at the beginning of the problem.

Teacher's Notes

This problem assumes that students can recognize decimals close to 0, $\frac{1}{2}$, and 1, which presumes a sound conceptual understanding of the meaning of decimal numerals. The problem extends students' understanding of decimals to estimation in multiplication. Students explore the effect of multiplying by decimals near 0, $\frac{1}{2}$, and 1 by examining patterns resulting from multiplication with each type of decimal. Encourage students to see the power of this estimation technique by having them estimate products of numbers that paper-and-pencil techniques would not easily accomplish.

Extensions

- Give students multiple-choice test items that involve multiplication with decimals, and have them identify how they can use estimation to select efficiently from among the available choices for answers without carrying out the calculation (e.g., by estimating the products and eliminating unreasonable responses).

- Give students a series of multiplication exercises involving decimal factors, and for each one, have students indicate products that are greater or less than the actual product. Leave a blank where the equal sign (=) would normally be, and have students insert either the "is less than" sign (<) or the "is greater than" sign (>) without calculating the value. The following is an example:

  Insert < or > into the square:

  1.0095 × 19.6 ☐ 19

- Give students a page of practice multiplication problems involving decimals, and tell them to do only those for which the answer is less than 1, or greater than 1, or about $\frac{1}{2}$, and so on.

Problem 6: Operations on a Fraction Number Line

(Adapted from *Developing Number Sense,* activity 24, p. 34 [Reys et al. 1992]; original source *Curriculum and Evaluation Standards for School Mathematics* [NCTM 1989])

Use the number line below to answer each of the following questions:

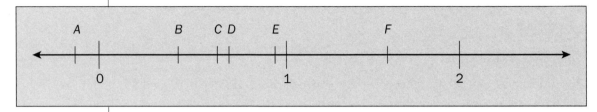

1. If you multiply the fractions represented by the points *D* and *E*, what point on the number line best represents the product? Explain.

2. If you multiply the fractions represented by the points *C* and *D*, what point on the number line best represents the product? Explain.

3. If you multiply the fractions represented by the points *B* and *F*, what point on the number line best represents the product? Explain.

4. What combinations of fractions represented by letters on the number line result in a product less than 1? Explain.

5. What general rules can you use to predict whether the product of any two fractions is less than 1?

Solutions to Problem 6

(Answers will vary, because students may estimate locations as plus or minus 0.1 of what the illustrative answers below indicate.)

(1) *D* looks like it could be 0.7, and *E* looks like it could be 0.9; and their product would be 0.63, which would be closest to *C* because that location looks like a little more than half.

(2) If *C* is 0.6 and *D* is 0.7, their product would be 0.42, which would be closest to *B*.

(3) *B* is close to one-half and *F* is close to one and one-half, so one-half of one and one-half is about three-fourths, which is closest to *D*.

(4) Any paired combination of *A, B, C, D, E,* and the combination of *A* and *F*. Points *B, C, D,* and *E* are all fractions less than 1, so when each is multiplied by another, their product will be less than 1. Because *A* is a negative number, any other positive factor used with *A* will result in a product that is less than 1 because it is negative. Also, because *A* is negative, multiplying it by *F* will result in a negative number, which is automatically less than 1 because *F* is positive.

(5) When multiplying two fractions or decimals less than 1, the product will always be less than 1. When multiplying a positive and a negative fraction or decimal, the product will be negative, making the answer always less than 1. When multiplying a number less than 1 by a number greater than 1, the size of the product will depend on the size of the factor greater than 1.

Teacher's Notes

This problem is useful for clarifying students' understanding of the effects of certain operations on fractions, and is excellent for prompting a class discussion. It originally appeared in *Curriculum and Evaluation Standards for School Mathematics* (NCTM 1989, p. 203). The problem assumes that students can locate decimals on the number line, and this ability may need to be assessed prior to beginning the work on the problems. Diagnostic assessment involves an ongoing process of listening to students' explanations and observing the connections that students make during class discussion, conducting dialogues with individual and small groups of students, and examining individual journal entries. For example, one teacher approached this problem by first having students identify the location of each letter. When the teacher asked about the location of B on the number line, the class dialogue went, in part, like the following:

Lauren:	It looks a little less than $1/2$, so I'll say $3/8$.
Scott:	I think that's a little too small: it's closer to $1/2$.
Teacher:	Scott, what makes you say $3/8$ is too small?
Scott:	Well, $3/8$ is 0.375, which is near $1/3$, and I think that B is closer to $1/2$ than $1/3$.
Al:	Is it OK to use decimals?

Such conversations reveal students' thinking, which can help teachers make informed decisions about subsequent instruction. This problem is particularly useful for assessing students' concepts of fractions and decimals on a number line, comparing and ordering fractions and decimals on a number line, and reasoning about rational number operations.

Extensions

- Have students predict the location of the quotient of any two letters on the number line. Do the same for sums and differences.

- Have students pose a sum, a difference, a multiplication, and a division problem that would result in an answer between 1 and F.

- Have students pose a sum, a difference, a multiplication, and a division problem that would result in an answer between A and 0.

Common Core Mathematical Practices

When students estimate and locate a product of two fractions indicated by location on a number line, they synthesize their understanding of fractions as represented on a number line, their ability to estimate the magnitude of each fraction, and their understanding of fractions multiplication. In their explanation for their answers, students **construct viable arguments and,** if they share these arguments with others, **critique the reasoning of others. Attention to precision** is crucial for effective mathematical communication in this activity.

Problem 7: Patterns with Fractions

(Adapted from *Patterns and Functions*, investigation 1, pp. 32–37 [Phillips et al. 1997])

For Grades 5 and 6

One day, the cookie monster sneaks into the kitchen and eats half a cookie; on the second day he comes in and eats half of what remains of the cookie from the first day; on the third day he comes in and eats half of what remains from the second day. If the cookie monster continues this process for seven days, how much of the cookie has he eaten? How much is left? If the process continues, will he ever eat all the cookie?

For Grades 7 and 8

A cricket is on the number line at the point labeled 0. She wants to get to the point labeled 1, but she can hop only half the remaining distance each time. Where on the number line is the cricket after seven hops? How much distance is left to go? Does the cricket ever get to the point labeled 1?

Solutions to Problem 7

How much of the cookie has the monster eaten in seven days? Where on the number line is the cricket after seven hops? $\frac{255}{256}$

How much is left after seven days? How much distance is left to reach the point at 1 after seven hops? $\frac{1}{256}$

Does the cookie monster ever eat all the cookie? Does the cricket ever get to the point labeled 1? Students are likely to argue that in reality it is impossible to keep subdividing the cookie or the number line, but ask them to use their "mind's eye" to imagine that they could. We can get as close to 1 as possible but can never eat the whole cookie or reach the point labeled 1 or beyond.

Teacher's Notes

For younger students (grades 5–6), tell the story of the cookie monster; for older students, tell the story of the cricket on the number line. The cookie context suggests a circle model. Plastic or paper circle-fractions parts can be helpful for modeling the solution, allowing students to rename the remaining part of the cookie as an equivalent fraction with halves, fourths, eighths, sixteenths, and so on. Together, model the amount of cookie eaten in the first two days. Encourage students to determine how much cookie was eaten each day and see how much was left. For the cricket version of the problem, the number line is the natural model to choose to illustrate the process of jumping half the distance each time, although students may need help in naming the appropriate points each time. After the second hop of one-half of one-half (then one-half of one-fourth), students have to add the new distance to the previous distance. They may be helped by renaming all the points on the number line each time to correspond with the size of the new additional distance. (For example, if the new hop is one-eighth of the full distance, all the previous points can be relabeled in eighths.)

In both versions of the problem, students can explore the subsequent iterations and quickly learn that the models get too small to represent with physical materials, and then they need to rely on their mind's eye to imagine the next iterations. To help students see patterns, have them organize their data in a table like the one in figure 1.1. Younger students might need help filling in the table, so the teacher may want to show the first two or three entries. As students fill the table in, have them explain how they went about trying to solve the problem. For example, some students will report looking at what is left each time and subtract this amount from the whole. Some students will see the pattern of halving, or that the denominator increases by a factor of 2 and the numerator is always one less than the denominator. Have them share what they see.

Common Core Mathematical Practices
When students make generalizations about repeated calculations—in this instance, figuring out how much is left after eating or traveling half the remaining amount—they *reason abstractly and quantitatively.*

Day	Amt. of Cookie Eaten	Sum	Amt. Not Eaten
Start		0	
1		$\frac{1}{2} = \frac{1}{2}$	$\frac{1}{2}$
2		$\frac{1}{2} + \frac{1}{4} = \frac{3}{4}$	$\frac{1}{4}$
3		$\frac{1}{2} + \frac{1}{4} + \frac{1}{8} = \frac{7}{8}$	$\frac{1}{8}$
4		$\frac{1}{2} + \frac{1}{4} + \frac{1}{8} + \frac{1}{16} = \frac{15}{16}$	$\frac{1}{16}$
5		$\frac{1}{2} + \frac{1}{4} + \frac{1}{8} + \frac{1}{16} + \frac{1}{32} = \frac{31}{32}$	$\frac{1}{32}$
6		$\frac{63}{64}$	
7		$\frac{127}{128}$	
8		$\frac{255}{256}$	
9		$\frac{511}{512}$	
10		$?$	
n	$\frac{1}{2} + \frac{1}{4} + \frac{1}{8} + \ldots + \frac{1}{2^n}$	$\frac{2^n - 1}{2^n}$	$\frac{1}{2^n}$

Fig. 1.1. Class-generated pattern for repeatedly halving the cookie

Enrich the discussion by having the students continue the pattern. What happens on day 10? Day 15? Reverse the process; ask, "On what day is only $\frac{1}{2048}$ of the distance left on the number line?" Students can use the chart or reason out the answer, using statements like, "Two raised to what power gives 2048?" or "How many twos must we multiply to get 2048?" Note that the pattern of the sums is an example of exponential growth, and the pattern of the amounts left is an example of exponential decay.

Elicit the sum associated with each day. Students can reply verbally, and you can write the sum symbolically next to the appropriate picture. Have the class generate the entries. It may be helpful to students if you rename each sum using a common denominator. Once students can verbally describe the pattern, help them generalize the pattern using symbols for the nth day:

$$\frac{1}{2}+\frac{1}{4}+\frac{1}{4}+\ldots+\frac{1}{2^n}=\frac{\left(2^n-1\right)}{2^n}.$$

Extensions

- Explore the behavior of the sum of the powers of $\frac{1}{3}$, the sum of the powers of $\frac{1}{4}$, and so on. (Exploring these sums with an area model, on a number-line model, and through calculations reveals that the sum of the powers of $\frac{1}{3}$ seems to approach $\frac{1}{2}$ and that the sum of the powers of $\frac{1}{4}$ seems to approach $\frac{1}{3}$.)

- Write a general algebraic expression to represent the sum of the powers of $\frac{1}{3}$, the sum of the powers of $\frac{1}{4}$, and so on.

Proportions

In this section, we use two problem contexts to engage students in real-world settings for proportional reasoning. The problems use whole-number and rational-number ideas to develop proportional ways of thinking. In particular, the problem Exploring the Size of a Million Dollars engages students in visualizing and manipulating large numbers, whereas Capture Recapture embeds concepts of proportional reasoning into the design of an experiment using a mathematical model.

Common Core Mathematical Practices

The two activities in this section require students to **make sense of problems and persevere in solving them.**

Problem 8: Exploring the Size of a Million Dollars

(Adapted from *Developing Number Sense*, activity 8, p. 22 [Reys et al. 1992])

Just as you decide to go to bed one night, the phone rings and a friend offers you a chance to become a millionaire. He tells you he won $2 million in a contest. The money was sent to him in two suitcases, each containing $1 million in one-dollar bills. He will give you one suitcase of money if your mom or dad will drive him to the airport to pick it up. Could your friend be telling you the truth? Can he make you a millionaire?

Materials

☑ Reams of paper

☑ Rulers

☑ A pan balance or scale

☑ Calculators

☑ Suitcase or duffel bag

Teacher's Notes

This problem presents an opportunity for small groups of students to work for a sustained period of time on a challenging problem involving proportional reasoning. Students typically take one of two approaches to the problem. The first uses volume, asking, "Can a standard suitcase hold $1,000,000 in one-dollar bills?" The second uses weight, asking, "Can a suitcase containing one million one-dollar bills be lifted?" After reading the problem to the students, tell them they will prepare a class presentation—on a transparency, on a poster board, or as a PowerPoint presentation—that makes a convincing case for or against the truth of the friend's statement. At first, students may expect the teacher to provide additional direction, but in fact, middle-grades students should already have the concepts and skills needed to solve this problem: an understanding of large numbers up to one million, computational and measurement estimation, and spatial visualization. The important aspects of problem solving include formulating problems, articulating assumptions, and testing and revising intermediate solutions. Have students solve the problem in small groups, and choose groups' members to represent a variety of strengths (e.g., a person who knows how to use a calculator and can interpret the reasonableness of results a calculator produces, a person who has a good sense of size and measurement, a person who is a good recorder or documenter). Diverse skills in team members can help them strengthen their final presentation.

Extensions

- If you could use larger denominations of bills (e.g., five-dollar or ten-dollar bills), what is the smallest everyday container that you would need to transport a million dollars?

Common Core Mathematical Practices
When students make a case for or against the truthfulness of the friend's claim about becoming a millionaire, they **construct viable arguments,** which in this activity requires that they **attend to precision.** When they present their cases, students will **critique the reasoning of others.**

- Use examples of foreign paper currency, preferably of different sizes, and have students refigure the problem for that currency. This activity may also involve changes in the denomination of the smallest bill and in the different sizes of the bills.

Problem 9: Capture Recapture

(Adapted from *Understanding Rational Numbers and Proportions,* activity 1, pp. 57–58, by Frances R. Curcio and J. Lewis McNeece [Curcio et al. 1994])

Given a shoebox of 80 to 100 cubes and a page of small sticky dots, have students do the following:

Tag Some Number of Cubes

1. Estimate the number of cubes in the box (without counting and without removing cubes from box). Write down your estimate.

2. Pull out one handful of cubes. Count them, and record the count in a table like the one below. Put a tag (sticky dot) on each one.

3. Return the cubes to the box, and mix the tagged cubes into the box of all cubes.

Recapture Some Number of Cubes

4. Record the trial number in a table like the one below (each pair of students should conduct at least five trials).

5. Pull out a handful of cubes.

6. Record the number of tagged cubes in this trial.

7. Record the *total* number of cubes pulled out in this trial.

8. Record the total number of cubes tagged in the whole box. (Notice that this number will not change. It will depend on the result in step 2 in the tagging above.)

9. Estimate the total number of cubes in the box. Use the given information you have and what you know about proportions. (Hint: How should the ratio of *recaptured tagged* to *recaptured total* compare with the ratio of *total tagged* to *total in the box*?)

10. Repeat steps 4–9 at least five times.

Trial Number	Number Tagged in This Recapture	Total Number Pulled in This Recapture	Number Tagged in the Whole Box	Estimated Total Number of Cubes

After completing five trials, answer the following questions:

- What is your estimate of the total number of cubes in the box? (Remind students that they all have the same number in the box.)

- Why do the estimated totals vary?

- Why would one expect the estimated totals to be fairly close to one another?

- How can statistics be used to combine the data from all the trials across your class to produce a better estimate?

Materials

☑ One shoebox for every pair of students in the class

☑ 80–100 cubes for every shoebox, the same number in every shoebox

☑ 20–30 small circular sticky dots to tag selected cubes in each shoebox

Teacher's Notes

The goal of this problem is to estimate the total number in a population by using proportions and extrapolating from a sample. In so doing, students use and deepen their knowledge of fraction concepts, ratios, proportion, equivalent fractions, decimals, percent, and mean (arithmetic average). Actually conducting the experiment using cubes helps students internalize the complexity of the problem.

In particular, this problem provides opportunities to connect rational numbers with proportion and statistics. In many situations, scientists employ rational-number concepts to make estimations and predictions based on data collected from representations of a population. For example, marine biologist Samuel Gruber from the University of Miami was studying the growth, movement, maturation, and reproduction of lemon sharks in Bimini Lagoon in the

1980s. One statistical technique that he used involved tagging sharks and then recapturing them. By using this capture-recapture technique, he was able to estimate the number of sharks in the lagoon by comparing the number of tagged sharks he recaptured with the total number of sharks he captured.

Extensions

- Samuel Gruber was a marine biologist at the University of Miami who studied lemon sharks. Gruber worked to estimate the number of sharks in Bimini Lagoon (Maddux 1986). Given that sharks in the lagoon tend to stay in the lagoon, and new sharks do not often enter the lagoon, how was Gruber able to use a capture-recapture method to estimate the number of sharks in the lagoon? Write up the steps that someone like Gruber would need to follow to conduct the investigation.

- Describe other situations in which one could use the capture-recapture method to estimate a population. Describe characteristics of situations that lend themselves to capture-recapture methods of estimating populations (e.g., closed system, moving objects, the existence of mixing, ability to tag objects somehow).

Exponents

This section uses the problem Patterns in the Powers Chart to illustrate how one can learn a great deal about and beyond number and operations by exploring number patterns. Overall, students "*discover* salient features of the pattern, *construct* understanding of the concepts and relationships, *develop* a language to talk about the pattern, *integrate,* and *discriminate* between the pattern and other patterns. When relationships between quantities in a pattern are studied, knowledge about important mathematical relationships and functions emerges" (Phillips et al. 1991, p. 1). Thus, in the problem below, students experience number and operations through problem solving and connections.

Problem 10: Patterns in the Powers Chart

(Adapted from *Patterns and Functions,* investigation 2, pp. 12–14 [Phillips et al. 1991])

Part 1: If we expand 2^{100}, what is the numeral in the units place?

Part 2: If we expand *any* whole number, 1 through 10, to the 100th power, what numeral is in the units place?

Solutions to Problem 10

Part 1: Since the exponent, 100, is a multiple of four, the units digit will be a 6.

Part 2: In 1^n the units digit is always 1; in 2^n the units digits cycle 2, 4, 8, 6; in 3^n the units digits cycle 3, 9, 7, 1; in 4^n the units digits cycle 4, 6; in 5^n the units digit is always 5; in 6^n the units digit is always 6; in 7^n the units digits cycle 7, 9, 3, 1; in 8^n the units digits cycle 8, 4, 2, 6; in 9^n the units digits cycle 9, 1; in 10^n the units digit is always 0.

Materials

☑ Calculators

Teacher's Notes

The purpose of this problem is to provide a problem-solving environment in which students can explore the concept of exponents and patterns associated with them. Prior to engaging in the problem, students should understand how to expand amounts expressed in exponential notation. Assess students' prerequisite knowledge by asking the following question:

> What digit is in the units place if you expand 2^{10}?
> ($2 \times 2 \times 2 \times 2 \times 2 \times 2 \times 2 \times 2 \times 2 \times 2 = 1024$, so 4 is the digit in the units place.)

Part 1

Begin the problem by having students explore ways in which they can solve the problem. If students use a scientific calculator, they may end up with scientific notation, which does not reveal the units place. Suggest using smaller exponents to find a pattern. Some students may use a table, such as the sample started below, to explore the patterns.

n	2^n
1	2
2	4
3	8
4	16

Common Core Mathematical Practices
By encountering the limitations of the scientific calculator on the activity, students learn about *using appropriate tools strategically.*

Pull the class together once students begin to discover that the units digits repeat in a cycle of four: 2, 4, 8, 6, 2, 4, 8, 6, …. Ask students the following questions:

- *When in the cycle does a 2 appear in the units place?* (For exponents of 1, 5, 9, …, in other words, for exponents that are one more than a multiple of 4 [or $4x + 1$], or some may notice for three less than a multiple of 4 [or $4x - 3$].)

- *When in the cycle does a 4 appear in the units place?* (For exponents of 2, 6, 10, … in other words, for exponents that are two more than a multiple of 4 [or $4x + 2$], or some may notice when the exponent is two less than a multiple of 4 [or $4x - 2$].)

- *When in the cycle does an 8 appear in the units place?* (For exponents of 3, 7, 11, … in other words, for exponents that are three more than a multiple of 4 [or $4x + 3$], or some may notice when the exponent is one less than a multiple of 4 [or $4x - 1$].)

- *When in the cycle does a 6 appear in the units place?* (For exponents of 3, 7, 11, … in other words, for exponents that are multiples of 4 [or $4x$].)

Finally, ask for the answer to part 1 of problem 10: *If 2^{100} is expanded, what is the digit in the units place?*

Part 2

When extending the search for patterns of the units digit to powers of all numbers 1 through 10, an amazing pattern emerges. The longest cycle for the units digit is four, and only 2, 3, 7, and 8 have a cycle of length four. A cycle of length one occurs for 1, 5, 6, and 10. A cycle length of two occurs for 4 and 9.

When we put this pattern into a table, we can observe other patterns (see table below). Some patterns to investigate are the endings for square numbers, those for cube numbers, or those that yield the same number. For example, ask the following questions:

- *Could 292 be a square?* (No, a square number does not end with a 2.)

- *What are the endings for numbers that are a fourth power?* (0, 1, 5, or 6)

- $2^4 = 4^2 = 16$. *Why?* (Factor both, and then see that their prime factorization is the same. $2^4 = 2 \times 2 \times 2 \times 2$ and $4^2 = 4 \times 4 = 2^2 \times 2^2 = [2 \times 2] \times [2 \times 2] = 2 \times 2 \times 2 \times 2$.) *Are there others?* (This discussion can lead to the generalization that $[2^n]^m = [2^m]^n$.)

Other investigations can lead to discovering the other exponential rules. For example, ask these questions:

- *Does $(2^2)(3^2) = 6^6$?* (No. Because $[2 \times 2] \times [3 \times 3]$ does not equal $6 \times 6 \times 6 \times 6 \times 6 \times 6$.)

Common Core Mathematical Practices

When students explore specific instances of $[2^n]^m = [2^m]^n$ and other rules for computing with exponents, they *look for and make use of structure.*

- *What is the exponent for the base 6 in $(2^2)(3^2) = 6^n$?* (The exponent is 2. Because $[2 \times 2] \times [3 \times 3] = 2 \times 2 \times 3 \times 3 = 2 \times 3 \times 2 \times 3 = [2 \times 3] \times [2 \times 3] = 6 \times 6 = 6^2$.)

n^1	n^2	n^3	n^4	n^5	n^6	Units Digits of the Powers
1	1	1	1	1	1	1
2	4	8	16	32	64	2, 4, 8, 6
3	9	27	81	243	729	3, 9, 7, 1
4	16	64	256	1,024	4,096	4, 6
5	25	125	625	3,125	15,625	5
6	36	216	1,296	7,776	46,656	6
7	49	343	2,401	16,807	117,649	7, 9, 3, 1
8	64	512	4,096	32,768	262,144	8, 4, 2, 6
9	81	729	6,561	59,049	531,441	9, 1
10	100	1000	10,000	100,000	1,000,000	0

Extensions

- What is the digit in the units place for 17^{100}? 24^{50}? 31^{10}? Note that these numbers will behave like 7, 4, and 1, respectively.

- How many zeros appear in 10^7? 10^{10}? 10^{100}?

- Which is larger: 6^{10} or 7^{10}? 8^{10} or 10^8? 6^9 or 9^6? Why?

- Try to find the missing numbers with one guess; check with a calculator.

$$?^7 = 823,543 \qquad ?^6 = 1,771,561 \qquad ?^5 = 371,293$$

(This question offers students a good opportunity to increase their estimation skills. In the first example, $823,543 < 10^7$, and the only numbers whose powers have a 3 in the units place must end in a 7 or 3. So the number is either 3 or 7, but closer to 7. Check this result on a calculator.)

- What is the largest power of 2 that can be displayed completely in the calculator window? (The answer will depend on the calculator being used.)

REFERENCES

Bezuk, Nadine. "From the File: Easy Pieces." *Arithmetic Teacher* 36 (February 1989): 3.

Curcio, Frances J., and Nadine S. Bezuk, with Barbara E. Armstrong, Alice F. Artzt, Heidi Janzen, Steven T. Klass, Tami Martin, J. Lewis McNeece, Claire M. Newman, Francine Sicklick, Susan B. Turkel, and Judith S. Zawojewski. *Understanding Rational Numbers and Proportions. Curriculum and Evaluation Standards for School Mathematics* Addenda Series, Grades 5–8. Reston, Va.: National Council of Teachers of Mathematics, 1994.

Maddux, Hilary C., ed. *The Challenge of the Unknown, Teaching Guide.* New York: W. W. Norton & Co., 1986.

National Council of Teachers of Mathematics (NCTM). *Curriculum and Evaluation Standards for School Mathematics.* Reston, Va.: NCTM, 1989.

Phillips, Elizabeth, with Theodore Gardella, Constance Kelly, and Jacqueline Stewart. *Patterns and Functions. Curriculum and Evaluation Standards for School Mathematics* Addenda Series, Grades 5–8. Reston, Va.: National Council of Teachers of Mathematics, 1991.

Reys, Barbara J., with Rita Barger, Maxim Bruckheimer, Barbara Dougherty, Jack Hope, Linda Lembke, Zvia Markovits, Andy Parnas, Sue Reehm, Ruthi Sturdevant, and Marianne Weber. *Developing Number Sense. Curriculum and Evaluation Standards for School Mathematics* Addenda Series, Grades 5–8. Reston, Va.: National Council of Teachers of Mathematics, 1992.

Measurement and Geometry

2

THE ACTIVITIES in this chapter derive from problems from two volumes in NCTM's Addenda series, Grades 5–8: *Geometry in the Middle Grades* and *Measurement in the Middle Grades*. We selected the problems for their potential to emphasize deep conceptual understanding, problem solving, and reasoning. We organized this chapter's problems into two parts—Measurement, and Visualizing and Representing Shapes.

Part 1: Measurement

Measurement is an intrinsic part of our everyday living. Whether we go shopping, attend a sports event, visit a bank, stay at home (e.g., doing carpentry, decorating, or working on hobbies), or even take a vacation (e.g., traveling and map reading), measurement is an integral part of our experiences. Modern technology depends wholly on measurement. Students should perceive mathematics as a discipline of reasoning that enables them to solve real-world problems, many of which include measurement.

Informal geometry and spatial thinking are vital aspects of the middle grades mathematics curriculum. Modeling, mapping, and engaging in activities and spatial experiences organized around physical phenomena can help students discover, visualize, and represent concepts and properties of geometric figures in the physical world. When given opportunities to create plans, build models, draw, sort, classify, and engage in geometric activities and mathematical creativity through problem solving, middle school students will experience the excitement and the challenge of learning geometry. Through geometric explorations and investigations, students develop spatial intuitions and an understanding of geometric concepts necessary to function effectively in a three-dimensional world. Geometry is a branch of mathematics rich in visual approaches to problem exploration, pattern finding, and reasoning in the middle grades, making it an appropriate platform for exploring other areas of mathematics.

Measurement is difficult to separate from a study of shapes and representations of geometric figures. Exploring length, area, and volume develops an understanding of shape and, at the same time, connects with other areas of mathematics and the physical world.

This section's first set of problems begins with estimating and measuring activities and then proceeds to activities that develop measurement formulas. Students then use these ideas to explore such important geometric relationships as the Pythagorean theorem and similarity. The problems in this section's second set include activities that develop students' visualization of three-dimensional shapes as two-dimensional representations, and vice versa. The section concludes with brief explorations of shape transformations on a plane. Many of the problems have natural connections with other areas of mathematics or have interesting applications; a problem's extensions usually explore both.

Introducing Measurement

If measurement is to be a useful tool, estimation becomes one of the important goals of teaching measurement. Estimation requires students to make a judgment of an object in relation to some standard. Extensive classroom experiences in estimation are needed so that students will develop estimation strategies…. Three common estimation strategies helpful to students include (1) having a model or referent (e.g., a doorknob is approximately one meter from the floor; (2) portioning a object to be estimated into parts for which students know the measure …; and (3) dividing up the object into a number of equal parts, called "unitizing."

—*Measurement in the Middle Grades*

The next few problems will use foregoing techniques.

Problem 1: Creating Metric ID Cards

(Adapted from *Measurement in the Middle Grades*, activity 4, pp. 12, 19 [Geddes et al. 1994])

Have you ever wondered how your height compares with your arm span? How much your school bag or shoes weigh? Some elementary school students were curious about such measurements, and they asked students in their school's middle grades to help them create a "metric ID card." The class generated the following list of information that might go on a metric ID card:

Name, date, school, grade, height, length of index finger, width of pinky finger, hand span, distance around head, arm span, distance from chin to fingertip, weight of backpack.

As a class, decide on what measurement information you would like to include on your cards.

- For each measurement, first make an estimate and then measure the object.

- Do you consistently overestimate or underestimate? Do you make better estimates on small objects or large ones?

- What adjustments would you make to the metric ID card, if any?

- Which measurements would you find useful for estimating lengths or distance—for instance, the length of a room or a book?

- Do any of the measurements on your metric ID card measure volume? If not, what measurement could you add that involves volume?

Materials

☑ Card stock to make metric ID cards

☑ Measuring tools, such as rulers, scales, string

Teacher's Notes

You can use this activity to assess students' understanding of the basic metric-system concepts. Being able to estimate measurement is an important part of students' understanding and skillful use of measurement.

You could introduce this activity by asking students which they think is greater—the distance around their neck, or that around their knee. Students could estimate each distance by putting their hands together around their necks and knees and judging how far their fingers overlap. They could then check their estimates by measuring each distance with a tape measure. Encourage students to share their strategies for estimating. For example, some students may know the length of their foot, which they can use to estimate distance. Some may use the sides of an 8 $\frac{1}{2}$-by-11-inch sheet of paper. Others may use the length of their thumbnail to measure smaller distances.

The set of measurements mentioned above for the metric ID card are suggestions. The class can pick a subset of those measures or add new ones, so long as everyone in the class uses the same set. Students can use these measurements for other activities in data and algebra, such as exploring the relationship between arm span and height. (See suggestions in the extensions.)

Extensions

For the first extension, the class may need to review the meaning of various types of *average,* including mean, median, and mode, and their appropriate uses. For example, they might conclude that the typical seventh grader is __ meters tall for a boy and __ meters tall for a girl. The average backpack (school bag) weighs _ grams, and so on. The last extension involves exploring the relationship between two numerical quantities—variables—displayed on a graph, which is an important concept in algebra.

- Explore various characteristics of a typical sixth-, seventh-, or eighth-grade student.

- Graph the class data for some of the measurements, for example, arm span versus height or height versus backpack weight. Describe the relationship between the two variables. How does this relationship show up in the graph?

Common Core Mathematical Practices
When students choose the appropriate measuring tools and judge the reasonableness of their estimates, they learn to *use appropriate tools strategically* and *attend to precision.*

Problem 2: How Big Is Your Foot?

(Adapted from *Measurement in the Middle Grades*, activity 5, pp. 12–13, 20 [Geddes et al. 1994])

Students who explored the previous problem wanted to add the length and size of their foot to the information gathered. They thought that the length would be easy to measure but were unsure how to measure the area of an irregular region. They decided to draw a copy of their foot on centimeter grid paper.

- Take your shoe off, and trace an outline of your foot on centimeter grid paper.

- How long is your foot (toe to heel)?

- How wide is your foot?

- What is the area of your foot? Explain how you counted the grid squares?

- Explain how to find the distance around your foot.

- Is it possible to get a more accurate estimate for length, width, and area of your foot? Explain.

Materials

☑ Optional: Blackline master 2.3

Solutions to Problem 2

Answers will vary. Students may use different methods for determining the area, and these should be discussed in class. To get a better estimate for lengths, students should suggest using a smaller unit, for instance, half-centimeter lengths. For area, a grid consisting of half-centimeter squares will lead to a better estimate.

Teacher's Notes

This problem's goal is to help students understand that area involves covering a region with square units, and that one can compute area by counting the number of square units it takes cover the region.

Some students may have difficulty counting regions that are not complete square units; you should encourage them to estimate and to put together regions whose areas add up to approximate one square unit. Look for different ways that students might count the squares, and discuss the approaches in class when the students discuss their explorations' results. For example, some students may each draw the largest rectangle they can within the boundaries of their foot, calculate that rectangle's area, and then count the remaining squares or parts of squares within the foot's boundaries. Other students may embed their foot in a rectangle, calculate that rectangle's area, and then subtract the area inside the rectangle that is outside the boundary of the foot.

Discuss sources of errors and how students could obtain more precise measurements. Using smaller units to measure a foot's area will give a more precise measurement. Using smaller units also lends greater precision to measuring lengths.

Extensions

- What is a typical foot size for boys and girls in this class? (Students could use their knowledge of mean, median, and mode to answer this question.)

- Does a relationship exist between a person's height and foot size? (Graphing the class's data on coordinate axes will help students explore this relationship.)

- Give students a copy of the outline of a small child's foot drawn on centimeter grid paper, as shown in figure 2.1. Ask each student to compare his or her foot's measurements with the child's, and have the class discuss the results. The discussion should enable the class to make several conjectures, such as "my foot is *x* times as long as the child's foot" or "*x* copies of the child's footprint will cover my footprint."

Common Core Mathematical Practices
When students share and discuss their strategies for estimating the area of a circle, they learn to **construct viable arguments and critique the reasoning of others.**

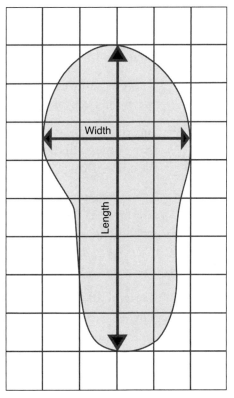

Fig. 2.1. A small child's footprint

Measuring Circles

Developing an understanding of the area of nonpolygonal regions, such as a circle, follows naturally from the counting and estimating techniques used in problem 2 above. The problems in this section involve both the area and circumference of a circle. The section ends with an interesting application.

Problem 3: Circumference of a Circle

(Adapted from *Measurement in the Middle Grades,* activity 12, pp. 32–33, 44 [Geddes et al. 1994])

Bicycle wheels, cans, and other round things (circles) come in many sizes. If you know the diameter of a circle (the longest distance across the circle), can you predict the circumference of (distance around) a circle?

- Measure the diameter of each circle and the circumference of each circle.

  Suggestion: Wrap a string around the circle, and then measure the length of the string. Record each measurement in a table with the following headings:

Object	Diameter (d)	Circumference (C)	$\dfrac{C}{d}$

- Describe any patterns in the table. Check your pattern by using a different circle.

- Use your pattern to write a rule that describes the relationship between the circumference of a circle and its diameter.

- Suppose you measure the diameter of a circle with a string. How many times will the string (diameter) fit into the circumference of the circle? Does your result agree with your conjecture?

- If the diameter of a bicycle wheel is 70 centimeters, approximately how far does the bicycle move in one revolution of the wheel? In ten revolutions?

Materials

☑ Circles of several different sizes, such as discs, bottoms of cylindrical cans, or paper circles

☑ Ruler

☑ String

☑ Calculators

☑ A tennis-ball can with three tennis balls for the extension

Common Core Mathematical Practices

When students observe patterns between the relationship of the diameter and circumference of a circle, and then use their conjecture to make predictions, they learn to **look for and make use of structure** and **reason abstractly and quantitatively.**

Solutions to Problem 3

- Students should observe that the ratio C/d is about 3. Most of the ratios should be close to 3.1. This number is called *pi* (π).

- The circumference is about three times the diameter, or $C = \pi d$.

- The diameter will fit into the circumference a bit more than three times.

- If the bicycle wheel's diameter is 70 centimeters, then its circumference is about 219.9 centimeters, or 2.199 meters. You would thus travel about 219.9 centimeters, or 2.199 meters, in one revolution and about 2199 centimeters, or 21.99 meters, in ten revolutions.

Teacher's Notes

In this problem students develop a formula for finding the circumference of a circle.

Start by making sure that students know how to measure the diameter and circumference of a circle. Groups of students should measure four or five different circles. They should then assemble data from the class and discuss patterns, noting that the ratio C/d is a bit more than 3, or 3^+. If students obtain ratios that are not reasonably close to 3, you might have students discuss possible reasons for these measurement discrepancies. Try to build insight and intuition by having students physically demonstrate with string that the length of the diameter of a circle fits around the circumference of the circle a little more than three times, that is $C \approx (3^+)d$. Once students have a sound understanding of that relationship, you can introduce π and the formula $C = \pi d$. Some students may be interested in the fact that π is an irrational number, meaning that its decimal representation does not repeat and goes on forever: $\pi = 3.141592654\ldots$. Mathematicians use computers to write π to more and more decimal places.

Extensions

- Express a circle's circumference in terms of its radius.

- Hold up a tennis ball can, which usually holds three tennis balls. Which is greater, the height or the circumference of the can? (Students usually guess the height, but you can use a string to demonstrate that the circumference is greater than the height.)

- Graph the relationship between the circumference of a circle and its diameter. Describe the relationship. (It is a linear function whose graph is a straight line with slope π.)

Common Core Mathematical Practices

When students graph the relationship between the circumference of a circle and its diameter and connect it to algebra, they learn to *reason abstractly and quantitatively.*

Problem 4: Area of Circles

(Adapted from *Measurement in the Middle Grades*, activity 12, pp. 32–33, 44 [Geddes et al. 1994])

Do part 1 first and then part 2.

Part 1

- Draw circles with radii 3 centimeters, 4 centimeters, and 5 centimeters on centimeter grid paper.

- Find the area of each circle. Describe how you found the area. Compare your strategies with those of your classmates.

Part 2

- As you compared strategies for finding the area of a circle with your classmates, you may have noticed that some strategies are more efficient than others. The following is an example:

Embed each of your circles from part 1 in a square on centimeter grid paper, as in figure 2.2. Draw two perpendicular diameters in each embedded circle, parallel to the grid lines, so that the diameters divide the original, embedded circle into four equal parts. The two diameters create four congruent squares, smaller than the original square but larger than the grid squares, within the square in which you embedded the circle, These four congruent squares are called *radius squares* (see fig. 2.2).

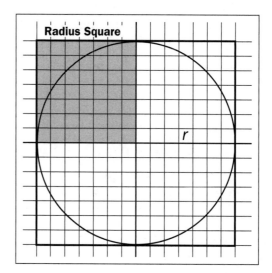

Fig. 2.2. One of four radius squares formed by perpendicular diameters in a circle

Is this name an appropriate description? Explain why.

- Record the following measurements in a table like the one shown.

Radius	Area of Radius Square	Number of Radius Squares Needed to Cover the Circle
3 cm		
4 cm		
5 cm		

- What is the area of each radius square?

- How is the area of a radius square related to the area of the circle?

- Approximately how many copies of one radius square will be needed to cover the circle?

- Suppose the radius of the circle is r; how does the area of the circle compare with area of the radius squares? That is, how many radius squares with side lengths r will be needed to cover the circle? Use this relationship to write a rule for the area, A, of a circle with radius r.

Materials

☑ Blackline master 2.3—two copies for each student

Common Core Mathematical Practices

When students observe patterns between the relationship of the radius and area of a circle and use their conjecture to make predictions, they learn to **look for and make use of structure** and **reason abstractly and quantitatively**.

Solutions to Problem 4

Part 1

- A circle with radius 3 cm has an area ≈ 28.3 cm². A circle with radius 4 cm has an area ≈ 50.3 cm². A circle with radius 5 cm has an area ≈ 78.5 cm².

- Strategies will vary. For example, some students will count each centimeter grid square or partial grid square inside the circle. Some will embed the circle in a square, count the grid squares outside the circle but inside the original, large square, and subtract the area of those regions from the area of the original square. Some will subdivide the circle into congruent sections, count the centimeter grid squares and partial grid squares inside one section, and then multiply by the number of congruent sections to get the circle's total area.

Part 2

- Students should find that a bit more than three radius squares are needed to cover the area of the circle. The area of each circle should be about $(3.1)r^2$, or close to πr^2.

Common Core Mathematical Practices

When students share their strategies with the class, they learn to construct *viable arguments and critique the reasoning of others.*

Teacher's Notes

The purpose of this problem is to develop a formula for finding the area of a circle with understanding.

You may want to save time by drawing the circles on centimeter grid paper and handing them out to the class. Remind students that area is the number of whole and partial square units needed to cover a figure. Let the students find the area of a circle using various counting strategies. They can each apply some of the strategies that they used for counting the area of their own foot in problem 2 to finding the area of a circle. For example, students may count each full square or part of a square in the first circle to find the area. Some may find more efficient ways to count, such as dividing the circle in half and counting the squares in one of the halves. The area of the circle is then twice the area of the half-circle. Dividing the circle into four equal parts by drawing two diameters through the center creates four congruent sectors. Finding the area of one sector and multiplying by four will give the area. Of course, students could then divide the circle into six, eight, and other numbers of congruent sectors to estimate its area.

Some students may embed the circle in a square, find the area of the square, and subtract the area of the regions that are inside the square but outside the circle. In this method, students should be able to visualize that the four regions that are inside the square but outside the circle are almost equal to one of the radius squares (see the diagram in fig. 2.3). Some students may cut out the four regions outside the circle and see how they compare with a radius square or with one of the quadrants of the circle.

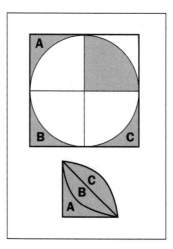

Fig. 2.3. Estimating the area of a circle as a little more than three radius squares

A little more than three radius squares will be needed to cover the circle. This method can be used to come up with a formula for finding the area of the circle. Students should conjecture that the area of the circle is approximately equal to three radius squares. This activity is a good occasion to remind students about pi (π) or to introduce pi if students are encountering it for the first time. Pi is a bit more than 3. Using the geometric representation seen in figure 2.3 is a good way for students to remember, or recall quickly, the area of a circle in subsequent situations.

The relationship between the area A of a circle and its radius r (i.e., $A = \pi r^2$) is important in algebra. It is a quadratic relationship whose graph is a parabola. Solving the equation for different values of the area or radius is an example of solving a simple quadratic equation. The relationship between the perimeter P of a circle and its radius r (i.e., $P = 2\pi r$) is an example of a linear relationship.

Extension

- Suppose the local pizza shop has a special offer: two 15-centimeter pizzas for $6 or one 30-centimeter pizza for $5. Which pizza is the better buy? Explain. (Answers will vary depending on whether students use circumference or area to make the comparisons.)

Problem 5: Grazing Cows

(Adapted from *Measurement in the Middle Grades,* activity 12, pp. 33, 45 [Geddes et al. 1994])

- A farmer tied his cow, Mooey, to a post with a rope 5 meters long. How many square meters of grazing ground does Mooey have? Explain your method for finding the answer.

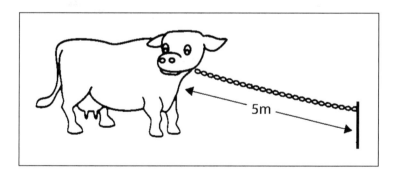

5m

- The farmer moves Mooey to another field and ties her to a post with the same rope at the corner of a closed shed 3 meters by 3 meters in the field. How many square meters of grazing ground does Mooey have? Explain your method for finding the area.

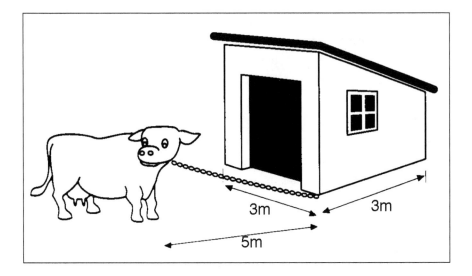

Materials

☑ Blackline master 2.5

Solutions to Problem 5

- The area is 25π, or about 78.5 square meters.
- The area in the second situation is (83/4)π, or about 65 square meters.

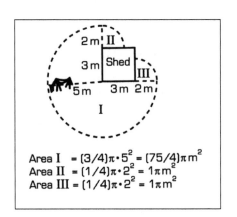

Area I = $(3/4)\pi \cdot 5^2 = (75/4)\pi\, m^2$
Area II = $(1/4)\pi \cdot 2^2 = 1\pi\, m^2$
Area III = $(1/4)\pi \cdot 2^2 = 1\pi\, m^2$

Teacher's Notes

This problem affords students an opportunity to apply their understanding of the area of a circle to a novel situation.

Students should realize that the solution to the first question is finding the area of circle with a radius of five meters. A common error made in solving the second situation is to find the area of the circle with radius five meters and then subtract the area of the shed, thus not realizing the constraints of Mooey's rope as it goes around the shed. The rope creates another, smaller circle. See the diagram given in Solutions to Problem 5 above.

Measuring Polygons

Students enter middle school with some knowledge of area and length. They may have encountered problems similar to questions 1 and 2 in problem 6 below. Some may even know the formula for finding the area and perimeter of a rectangle. You can use this section's problems (1) to strengthen students' understanding of area of polygons or (2) to develop the formulas for those areas if students have not done so themselves in previous grades.

The problems in this section explore the area and length of figures drawn on a square-dot grid paper. We will restrict some but not all the problems to a five-dot-by-five-dot grid. For convenience, we refer to this representation as square-dot paper. In the first problem, students explore the area of irregular figures on square-dot paper.

Students can draw line segments and squares on the grid by connecting the points on the grid. The smallest possible square drawn between grid points has a side length of 1 unit and an area of 1 square unit. Some squares that students can draw on the dot paper will not be horizontal or vertical. In these instances, students will need to use the strategy of counting the grid squares contained in the drawn square to determine the latter's area. The areas of the squares in figure 2.4 below, from left to right, are 1 square unit, 2 square units, and 4 square units. The lengths of each square's side, from left to right, are

$$1 \text{ unit}, \sqrt{2} \text{ units, and } 2 \text{ units.}$$

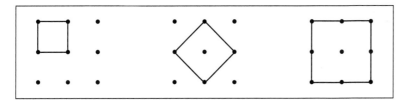

Note: Some schools may have geoboards that students could use for these problems. A geoboard, a square board with twenty-five pegs evenly spaced in five rows and five columns, is a physical model for a five-dot-by-five-dot grid. Students can create line segments and area on the geoboard with a rubber band and use the geoboard with blackline master 2.4.

Problem 6: Areas of Polygons

(Adapted from *Measurement in the Middle Grades*, activity 10, pp. 31, 40 [Geddes et al. 1994])

1.   Find the area of figures A, B, C, and D below. Show how you found the area.

2. The figure below has two holes (shaded regions). Find the area of the figure.

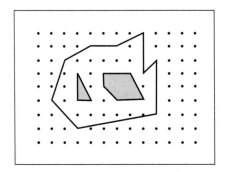

3. On square-dot paper, create a rectangle 3 units by 2 units. Divide the rectangle into two regions that have the same area. Find as many different ways as you can to do this.

Materials

☑ Blackline master 2.4, or 2.6, which repeats these problems—one copy for each student

☑ Optional: geoboards

Solutions to Problem 6

1. Figure A: *Area* = 6 square units; figure B: *Area* = 8 square units; figure C: *Area* = 5 square units; figure D: *Area* = 5 square units.

2. A = 32.5 square units.

3. Answers will vary. Some possibilities are the following:

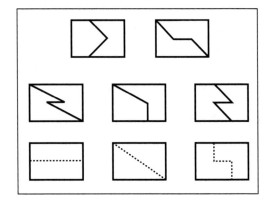

Teacher's Notes

In this problem, students continue to explore area on a geoboard or square-dot paper, including the areas of irregularly shaped figures. This problem requires students to use their understanding of a figure's area as the count of unit squares needed to cover the figure. Students may use strategies similar to those used in problems 2 and 5. The difference in this activity is that students can get a more exact answer because the nonrectangular parts are usually half a square or rectangle whose area they can easily compute.

Look for strategies that students use to find the areas. Some may subdivide a figure into rectangles, squares, or right triangles. Others may enclose the figure in a rectangle or square and subtract the area outside the figure from the area of the rectangle. In the last question, students may need an example or two to get started.

Extension

- Explore the relationship among the boundary points B, interior points I, and the area A of a figure drawn on square-dot paper. (The relationship is $A = [1/2B] + [I - 1]$, where A is the area, B is the number of points on the boundary, and I is the number of points in the interior. This relationship is called Pick's formula. Note that this formula works only for figures without holes. Figures with holes require a different formula, $A = [1/2B] + [I - 1] + H$, where H is the number of holes and the figure's total number of boundary points B includes the boundary points of the holes.)

Problem 7: Area of Squares and Square Roots

(Adapted from *Measurement in the Middle Grades*, activity 11, pp. 31–32, 42 [Geddes et al. 1994])

- Find all the squares that you can draw on a five-dot-by-five-dot grid.

- Label each square with its area. Explain how you found your squares and their areas.

- Find the length of the side of each square.

Materials

☑ For every student, one copy of blackline master 2.1 or several copies of blackline master 2.2

☑ Optional: geoboards

Common Core Mathematical Practices
When students share and explain their strategies for finding the area of the figures, they are learn to **construct viable arguments and critique the reasoning of others.**

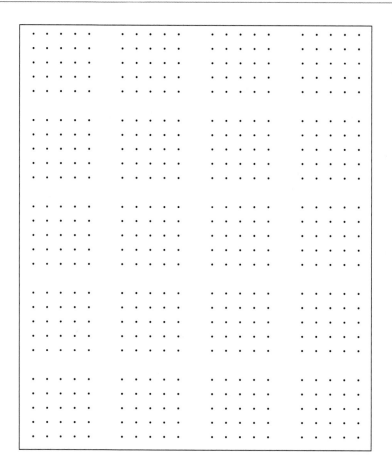

Solutions to Problem 7

- The squares that are possible on a five-square-by-five-square dot grid are as follows:

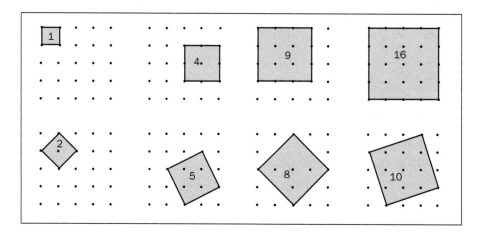

- The area of the squares are, respectively, 1, 4, 9, 16, 2, 5, 8, and 10.
- The lengths of the sides of the squares are, respectively, 1, 2, 3, 4, $\sqrt{2}$, $\sqrt{5}$, $\sqrt{8}$, and $\sqrt{10}$.

Teacher's Notes

In this problem, students continue to explore the relationship of the area of a square on square-dot paper and the length of a side of the square. Finding the length of a side involves irrational numbers. This problem can serve as an introduction to square roots and irrational numbers if your class has not studied them.

Discuss various strategies for drawing a square and determining its area. For the squares that are not in vertical orientation on the square-dot paper, students may notice that if they start with a slant line, it has a slope that is determined by counting the number of units it slants up and over from the starting point. Therefore, to find the next consecutive side, one can count over the same number of units and down the same number of units. Students will most likely not use slope, but they may notice that the up-and-over move is describing a right triangle whose hypotenuse is the slant line. Ask which squares were easy to find and which were not. Also, have students explain why the figures they drew were squares.

Most students will not be able to find the length of the side of a square with nonvertical or nonhorizontal sides unless they have studied square roots. In these situations, students will find the area by counting unit squares that cover the square. If students have studied similarity, they might notice that once they have created a square whose area is 2 square units, doubling the length of its side increases its area by a factor of 4. This new square will have an area of 8 square units.

To find the lengths of the sides of the squares, some students who have studied square roots may realize that some of the sides have irrational lengths. If your class has not studied square roots, this activity is a good opportunity to introduce them. You might do so as follows: The area of a square with side length s is $s \times s$, or s^2. For example, a square with length 2 units has an area of 4 square units. Suppose a square has an area of 9 square units; its side length is 3 units, because $3 \times 3 = 9$. Suppose a square has an area of 2 square units; what is its side length? We know that $2 \times 2 = 4$ and $3 \times 3 = 9$, so the length must be greater than 2 but less than 3. If we try various numbers between 2 and 3, none of them when multiplied by itself equals 2. In fact, no rational number of the form a/b, where a and b are whole numbers, when multiplied by itself equals 2. We define the length of the side of square with area 2 to be

$$\sqrt{2},$$

which is an example of an irrational number. Other examples of irrational numbers are

$$\sqrt{3}, \sqrt{5}, \sqrt{6}, \text{ and } \sqrt{8}.$$

Common Core Mathematical Practices

When students share and explain their strategies for finding the area of the figures on a 5-by-5-dot grid by counting square units, they are learning to *use appropriate tools strategically.*

The decimal representation of an irrational number is a nonrepeating decimal that does not terminate. For example,

$$\sqrt{2} = 1.41421356\ldots, \sqrt{3} = 1.75205080\ldots.$$

Extensions

- Locate on a number line the lengths of the sides of the squares that can be drawn on a geoboard.

- Find the two consecutive whole numbers that each of the following square roots is between:

$$\sqrt{7}, \sqrt{3}, \sqrt{11}, \sqrt{20}.$$

Problem 8: Finding Lengths of Line Segments

(Adapted from *Measurement in the Middle Grades,* activity 11, pp. 31–32, 42 [Geddes et al. 1994])

- Find the lengths of all line segments that can be drawn on a five-dot-by-five-dot square grid.

- Which lines have a length between 2 and 3? Between 3 and 5?

- Which lines have a length greater than 5?

- One student claimed that the length of one of the line segments is

$$2\sqrt{2}.$$

Is this length possible? Explain.

Materials

☑ Several copies of blackline master 2.2 *or* one copy of blackline master 2.1 for each student

☑ Optional: geoboards

Teacher's Notes

In the previous problem, students found that some squares have lengths that are not rational numbers; those lengths are irrational numbers. In this problem, students will continue to look at the lengths of other line segments that they can draw on a five-dot-by-five-dot grid.

Solutions to Problem 8

- Lengths of lines on a five-square-by-five-square dot grid are 1, 2, 3, 4, 5, $\sqrt{2}$, $\sqrt{8}$, $\sqrt{18}$, $\sqrt{32}$, $\sqrt{5}$, $\sqrt{20}$, $\sqrt{13}$, $\sqrt{10}$, and $\sqrt{17}$.

- The length $\sqrt{2}$ is between 1 and 2.

- The lengths $\sqrt{5}$ and $\sqrt{8}$ are between 2 and 3. The lengths $\sqrt{18}$, $\sqrt{20}$, $\sqrt{13}$, $\sqrt{10}$, and $\sqrt{17}$ are between 3 and 5.

- The length $\sqrt{32}$ is greater than 5.

- The square with area 8 square units can be created from a square whose area is 2 square units by doubling the length of its side, which is $2\sqrt{2}$. The area of the new square is 8, and its side length is $\sqrt{8}$. Therefore, $\sqrt{8} = 2\sqrt{2}$.

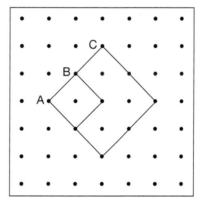

Students may find the lengths by first drawing a square on the line segment, finding the area of the square, and then taking the square root of the area to find the length of the side of the square. To do so, they may have to extend the five-by-five dot grid because some squares may not fit on it. For example, if students draw the line in figure 2.5a on the square dot grid, they will have to extend the grid as in figure 2.5b to show the square that can be built with this length. The square has an area of 25 square units. Therefore, the length of its side (the original line segment) is

$$\sqrt{25}, \text{ or } 5, \text{ units.}$$

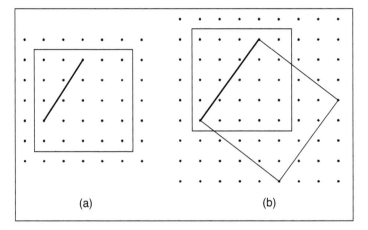

Fig. 2.5. Finding the length of a side of a square on a dot grid

These procedures are getting students ready to explore the Pythagorean theorem, which states that the sum of the areas of the squares built on the legs of a right triangle is equal to the area of the square built on the hypotenuse. (See problem 9.)

To be sure that all the line segments have been found, encourage students to find a systematic way to keep track of the line segments. An example is seen in figure 2.6.

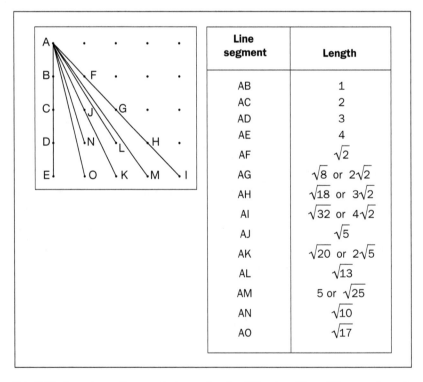

Line segment	Length
AB	1
AC	2
AD	3
AE	4
AF	$\sqrt{2}$
AG	$\sqrt{8}$ or $2\sqrt{2}$
AH	$\sqrt{18}$ or $3\sqrt{2}$
AI	$\sqrt{32}$ or $4\sqrt{2}$
AJ	$\sqrt{5}$
AK	$\sqrt{20}$ or $2\sqrt{5}$
AL	$\sqrt{13}$
AM	5 or $\sqrt{25}$
AN	$\sqrt{10}$
AO	$\sqrt{17}$

Fig. 2.6. A systematic way to keep track of the lengths of line segments on a dot grid

Other questions to ask students are the following:

- Can other lengths be expressed in two ways like $2\sqrt{2}$ and $\sqrt{8}$?

- Between what two consecutive whole numbers does $\sqrt{32}$ lie?

- On square-dot paper draw a line segment whose length is $\sqrt{29}$. Draw another line segment on square-dot paper, and find its length. Locate the lengths of the sides on a number line.

Extensions

- Draw a right triangle on square-dot paper. What are its area and perimeter?

- On square-dot paper draw a nonrectangular parallelogram with an area of 6 square units. What is its perimeter? Is your parallelogram the same as those of your classmates? Explain why or why not.

- On square-dot paper draw a triangle with an area of 5 square units. What is its perimeter? Is your triangle the same as those of your classmates? Explain why or why not.

- Create an irregular figure on square-dot paper, and find its area and perimeter.

Problem 9: Squares and the Pythagorean Theorem

(Adapted from *Measurement in the Middle Grades,* activity 11, number 2, pp. 31–31, 42 [Geddes et al. 1994])

A right triangle is a triangle with one right angle. The two sides that form the right angle are called the *legs* of the triangle. The side opposite the right angle is called the *hypotenuse.*

- On dot-grid paper, draw a right triangle with legs whose lengths are each one unit.

- Draw a square on the legs and hypotenuse of the triangle. What is the area of each square?

- Continue to explore other right triangles with different length legs. Find the areas of the squares built on the legs and hypotenuse. Record these results in a table like the following:

Length of Leg 1	Length of Leg 2	Area of Square on Leg 1	Area of Square on Leg 2	Area of Square on Hypotenuse
1	1			
1	2			
2	2			
1	3			
3	4			

- If the lengths of the legs of a right triangle are called *a* and *b,* what conjecture can you make about the relationship of the areas of the squares on the two legs to the area of the square on the hypotenuse with length *c?* (This conjecture is called the Pythagorean theorem, after the famous Greek mathematician Pythagoras, who Western history first credits with discovering and proving it.)

- Explain how you can use this conjecture to find the length of the hypotenuse of the triangles in the table. Use examples in your explanation.

Materials

☑ Blackline master 2.1—one copy for each student

Solutions to Problem 9

- For a triangle whose legs are each 1 unit, its hypotenuse is $\sqrt{2}$ units, and $1^2 + 1^2 = \left(\sqrt{2}\right)^2$.

Length of Leg 1	Length of Leg 2	Area of Square on Leg 1	Area of Square on Leg 2	Area of Square on Hypotenuse
1	1	1	1	2
1	2	1	4	5
2	2	4	4	8
1	3	1	9	10
3	4	9	16	25

Solutions to Problem 9—Continued

- The Pythagorean theorem states that the sum of the area of the squares on the legs of a right triangle is equal to the area of the square on the hypotenuse. If a and b are the lengths of the legs and c is the length of the hypotenuse, then $a^2 + b^2 = c^2$. See figure 2.7.

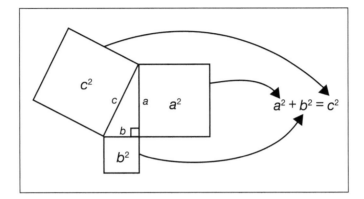

Fig. 2.7. Geometric interpretation of the Pythagorean theorem

Teacher's Notes

This problem strengthens students' understanding of area by looking for patterns and making a conjecture about the relationship between the side lengths of a right triangle and the squares drawn on its sides. This geometric interpretation of the relationship develops an understanding of the Pythagorean theorem and provides an important connection between algebra and geometry. The next problem explores a geometric proof of this conjecture.

Introduce the problem by drawing a right triangle whose side lengths are 1 unit on square-dot paper. Ask someone from the class to draw the squares on the legs and hypotenuse of the triangle (see fig. 2.8). Solicit strategies for finding the area of each square. Record the information in a table. Encourage the class to look for patterns as they work on other right triangles.

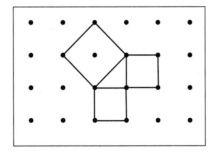

Fig. 2.8. Drawing squares on the legs and hypotenuse of a right triangle with side lengths 1 unit

Common Core Mathematical Practices

When students explore the relationship between the side lengths of a right triangle and the squares drawn on its sides, observe patterns, and make a conjecture about the relationship, they learn to *look for and express regularity in repeated reasoning.*

Problem 10: Proving the Pythagorean Theorem

(Adapted from *Measurement in the Middle Grades*, activity 11, pp. 31–32, 43 [Geddes et al. 1994])

Figure 2.9 shows squares drawn on the sides of a right triangle with side lengths 1, 2, and $\sqrt{5}$. The figure subdivides the square on the hypotenuse into smaller figures.

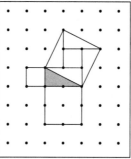

Fig. 2.9. Squares drawn on the sides of a right triangle with
side lengths 1, 2, and $\sqrt{5}$

- Describe each piece.

- Cut out the five pieces of the square of the hypotenuse, and reassemble the five pieces so that they fill the squares on the two legs of the right triangle. Is this task possible? Why or why not?

- Repeat the previous step for the other right triangle on the activity sheet. Is your conjecture still true? Explain.

- Explain how this process proves that the Pythagorean theorem is true.

Materials

☑ Blackline master 2.7—one copy for each student

Teacher's Notes

This problem gives students an opportunity to prove a conjecture. The geometric proof enhances students' understanding of the Pythagorean theorem.

Students may need help describing the pieces that make up the square on the hypotenuse. The pieces should fit in the two smaller squares so that no two pieces overlap and no empty spaces result. This procedure shows that the area of the square on the hypotenuse equals the sum of the area of the squares on the legs. Since this procedure can be applied to any right triangle, it is a proof for the Pythagorean theorem. Students may be interested to know that more than 300

Solution to Problem 10

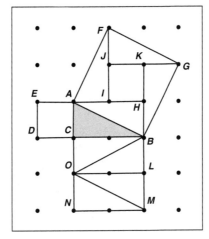

different proofs for this theorem exist and that Pythagoras developed his proof for this theorem in the sixth century BCE.

As an extra challenge, some students may want to try another right triangle. Subdividing the square on △*ABC*'s hypotenuse, *AFGB*, will require some knowledge about the relationships among the smaller congruent triangles △*AFI*, △*FGJ*, △*GBK*, and △*ABH*; the small square *HIJK*; and the squares *BMNC* and *ACDE* on △*ABC*'s legs.

Extensions

- Use the Pythagorean theorem to find the length of the hypotenuse of a right triangle whose leg lengths are 6 units and 2 units. (The length is $\sqrt{40}$, or $2\sqrt{10}$, units.)

- Use the Pythagorean theorem to find the length of the leg of a right triangle whose hypotenuse has a length of 7 units and one leg has a length of 4 units. (The length of the missing leg is $\sqrt{33}$ units.)

- Explain how to find the missing lengths of sides of a right triangle if you have forgotten the Pythagorean theorem.

  (Students might go back to the square-dot paper and draw a square on the missing side, find its area, and then use the area to find the side length.)

- Explain how to find the distance between two points on a dot grid or coordinate grid.

  (If the line is vertical or horizontal, you can determine the lengths by counting. If it is a slant line, then you can think of this line as

Common Core Mathematical Practices
When students provide a proof for the Pythagorean theorem using a geometric argument, they learn to *construct viable arguments and critique the reasoning of others.*

a hypotenuse of a right triangle. To find the lengths of the sides, you can use the coordinates of the endpoints of the slant line. Use these lengths and the Pythagorean theorem to find the length of the hypotenuse. Later, in high school, students will see that they can capture this procedure by the formula

$$d = \sqrt{\left(x_1 - x_2\right)^2 + \left(y_1 - y_2\right)^2},$$

where d is the distance between two points whose coordinates are (x_1, y_1) and (x_2, y_2). Alternatively, you could label several points on grid paper and ask students to find the length of the line segment between each pair of points.)

- Describe how you would draw a line segment on a grid whose length is $\sqrt{45}$ units.

(Students might use a guess-and-check method to find the two square numbers whose sum is 45 units, which are 36 and 9. From this result, they can determine that leg lengths of 6 and 3 units will give a right triangle with hypotenuse of length $\sqrt{45}$ units.)

- Find several sets of three whole numbers that satisfy the Pythagorean theorem. (These sets of whole numbers are called *Pythagorean triples*. A classic example is a right triangle with side lengths 3, 4, 5, because $3^2 + 4^2 = 5^2$. Another example is the triple 5, 12, 13. Also, multiplying all three whole numbers in a Pythagorean triple by the same whole number will create a Pythagorean triple. For example, 6, 8, and 10 is a Pythagorean triple, as is 15, 20 and 25, and so on.)

Problem 11: Using the Pythagorean Theorem

(Adapted from *Measurement in the Middle Grades,* activity 11, pp. 31–32, 43 [Geddes et al. 1994])

The Pythagorean theorem is useful for solving a variety of problems, as in the following situations:

- If a field is 14 meters by 48 meters, how many meters will you save if you run diagonally across the field instead of running around the two sides of the field? Explain.

- Can a circular table top 3 meters in diameter fit through a doorway with dimensions 1 meter by 2.9 meters? Explain.

- A ladder 8 meters long is leaning against the wall of a house. The foot of the ladder is 2 meters from the wall. How high up on the wall does the ladder reach? Explain.

Common Core Mathematical Practices

When students apply their knowledge of the Pythagorean theorem to new situations, they develop deeper understanding of the theorem and learn to *reason abstractly and quantitatively.*

- Is it possible to store a bamboo pole 3 meters long in a closet 1 meter by 2 meters by 2.5 meters? Explain.

- If someone gave you the following set of directions, how many paces (steps), measured in a straight line, are you away from your starting point? Explain. Assume that each pace (step) is the same length:

  Go forward 8 steps, continue to face the same direction and go left 7 steps, right 5 steps, left 12 steps, right 3 steps, left 4 steps.

Solutions to Problem 11

- The diagonal is 50 meters, so you save 12 meters.

- Yes, the table will fit. The diameter is 3 meters, which makes it too long to go through in a vertical position, but it will just fit through in a slant (hypotenuse formed by the side and bottom of the door) position because the slant distance is about 3.07 meters.

- The height is $\sqrt{60}$ meters.

- Yes, because the diagonal of the closet is about $\sqrt{11.25}$, or a bit more than 3, meters, the 3-meter pole will fit on a slant. Note that if you change the length of the pole to 3.5 meters, it will not fit in the closet.

- The distance from the starting point is 17 steps. It is the length of the hypotenuse formed by the two sides—one, the 8 steps forward; the other, the total distance going left and right, or 15 steps).

Teacher's Notes

This problem gives students an opportunity to apply their understanding of the Pythagorean theorem to solve interesting problems.

You could assign different problems to different groups of students to work out. Let each group present its findings. Drawings and calculations should accompany each presentation.

Measuring Surface Area and Volume

Problem 12: Surface Area

(Adapted from *Measurement in the Middle Grades*, activity 14, pp. 33–34, 47 [Geddes et al. 1994])

A gift you bought for a friend is in a rectangular box 40 centimeters by 30 centimeters by 10 centimeters (see fig. 2.10). You decide to cover all six sides of the box with gold foil to make it look attractive. How much gold foil will you need to cover the box? Explain.

Common Core Mathematical Practices
When students use their understanding of the Pythagorean theorem to solve problems arising in daily life, they learn to *model with mathematics.*

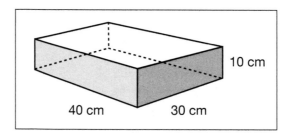

Fig. 2.10. Gift box to be covered with gold foil

Materials

☑ Optional—cardboard boxes

☑ One copy of blackline master 2.3 for each student

Solution to Problem 12

The amount of foil needed to cover the box is—
$2[(40 \times 10) + (40 \times 30) + (10 \times 30)]$ or $2(40 \times 10) + 2(40 \times 30) + 2(10 \times 30) = 3800$ cm^2.

Teacher's Notes

You can use this problem to help students develop a formula for finding the surface area of a rectangular prism. To introduce the problem, hold up a box and have students identify the box's features, that is, its sides, or *faces*. Explain that you want to cover these faces with foil. Let students explore for few minutes to see if they recognize that they need to find the sum of the areas of the box's faces. If students are having trouble, ask them if they see any relationships among the faces (rectangles) of the box. (There are three sets of two congruent rectangles each.) You might have some small cardboard boxes available for them to cut apart to visualize the pattern of the surface area and how this pattern folds to become a box. To reinforce their understanding of area, some students could trace the faces of the box on centimeter grid paper and then determine the area of each face. Ask them, "What is the sum of the areas of the box's faces?"

Give students a couple of more boxes to check their method. Ask the following:

> Suppose the dimensions of a rectangular prism (box) are the height, h; length, l; and width, w. Express the total area of a rectangular prism's faces in terms of h, l, and w (see fig. 2.11).

If you are using this problem to develop an understanding of surface area, tell students at this time that the amount of material needed to cover the sides of the box or rectangular prism is called the figure's *surface area*.

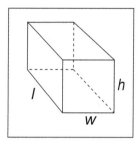

Fig. 2.11. Rectangular prism

Extension

- Suppose your gift was a cylindrical can of tennis balls. The surface area of the can (cylinder) is the sum of the area of the rounded surface of the cylinder (called the *lateral surface*) and the areas of the two bases. What is the surface area of the cylinder? (Using a cylindrical can will help students make a pattern of the surface area. They can cut a small juice can apart to form a pattern, then measure the tops and sides. The physical model will help them visualize that the lateral surface of a cylinder forms a rectangle. The dimensions of the rectangle are the height of the can and the circumference of a base. After a few examples, students should be able to generalize that the surface area of a cylinder is the sum of the areas of the two circular bases and the area of the lateral side. If the radius of the bases is r and the height of the cylinder is h, then the total surface area is $2\pi r2 + 2\pi rh$ [see fig. 2.12].)

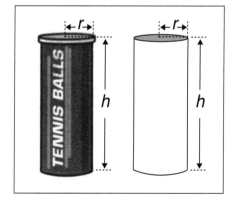

Fig. 2.12. Cylindrical tennis ball can

Common Core Mathematical Practices
When students use boxes and cans to develop understanding and a formula for finding surface area, they *learn to model with mathematics.*

Problem 13: Volume

(Adapted from *Measurement in the Middle Grades,* activity 15, pp. 34–35, 49 [Geddes et al. 1994])

A rectangular box has a height of 3 centimeters, a width of 4 centimeters, and a length of 5 centimeters (see fig. 2.13). If you wanted to fill the box with centimeter cubes, how many would you need? Explain.

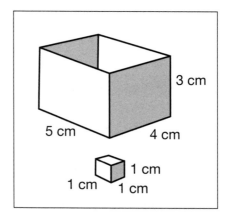

Fig. 2.13. Filling rectangular prisms with unit cubes to introduce volume

Materials

☑ Small rectangular boxes, clear plastic boxes, grid paper, unit cubes

☑ For the extensions, cylinders, pyramids, and cones

Solution to Problem 13

The number of centimeter cubes needed to fill the box is sixty (60). Students may use various strategies, but as they fill the box with unit cubes, some observe that it holds three layers of twenty unit cubes.

Teacher's Notes

You can use this problem to help students develop a formula for finding the volume of a rectangular prism. Hold up a small, rectangular box. Have the students describe how to find the dimensions of the box. Tell them that the box is also a rectangular prism. Ask how these dimensions relate to features (faces) of the rectangular prism. Let students explore the problem. Look for strategies that they use to fill and count the contents of the box. Some students may realize that filling the box with centimeter cubes means filling the box one layer at a time with the cubes. The number of unit cubes in each layer is the same as the area of the base, or $l \times w$. The number of layers needed to fill the box is equal to the height, h.

Therefore the volume is $l \times w \times h$. Using a transparent box or one made from transparent grid paper is a great way for students to see the box filling up one layer at time.

Give students another rectangular prism, and have them find its volume without filling it with unit cubes. They will need a ruler to measure the dimensions. If you have enough unit cubes, they can check their answer by filling the prism with unit cubes.

This method of finding the volume of a rectangular prism is the same for any prism (triangular, hexagonal, and so on) and cylinders. See the extensions that follow.

Extensions

- Find a formula for the volume of a cylinder. (The method for finding the volume of a cylinder is the same as that for a rectangular prism. That is, you can determine a cylinder's volume by stacking unit cubes in layers in the cylinder. The number of cubes needed is the area of the base times the height of the cylinder. If the height is h and the radius of the base is r, then the volume is $\pi r^2 h$. Clear plastic cylinders are great tools for helping students form visual images for the meaning of volume—the number of unit cubes needed to fill a container. Bear in mind, however, that unit cubes can't completely fill a cylinder, so the solutions students reach will be approximations.

- Find a formula for the volume of a pyramid. (You can determine a pyramid's volume by comparing its volume with that of a rectangular prism with the pyramid's same base and height. A pyramid's is one-third that of the rectangular prism.)

- Find a formula for volume of a cone. (You can find a cone's volume by comparing its volume with that of a cylinder with the cone's same height and radius. The cone's volume is one-third that of the cylinder.)

  Note: Filling plastic containers in these shapes with liquid or rice and comparing volumes makes for a compelling argument about the relationships between pyramids and rectangular prisms and between cones and cylinders.

- In a lumberyard, you see plywood sheets stacked straight up. Nearby, you see another, slanted stack of the same number and size of plywood sheets (see fig. 2.14). Which stack has the greater number of cubic meters of wood? Try this with a stack of index cards arranged in straight stacks, slanted stacks, and spiral stacks, each stack having the same number and size of cards. Which stack has the greatest volume? Explain.

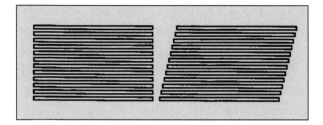

Fig. 2.14. Two stacks of plywood sheets to compare volume

- Repeat the experiment above with stacks of crackers of different shapes—a triangle, square, hexagon, and circle. These stacks, in that order, represent a triangular prism, square prism, hexagonal prism, and circular cylinder.

- Take two sheets of identical paper (e.g., 8.5 inches by 11 inches). Roll one sheet vertically and the other sheet horizontally, and tape each to form a right circular cylinder. If you were to fill each with popcorn, would they contain the same amount of popcorn? Explain and justify your reasoning.

(For an 8.5-by-11-inch sheet, the cylinder with height 8.5 inches will have a volume of approximately 82 cubic inches, and the cylinder with height 11 inches will have a volume of approximately 63 cubic inches. For a dramatic visual comparison of the volumes, put the taller cylinder inside the shorter cylinder as in figure 2.15. Fill the taller cylinder with popcorn, and slowly lift it out of the shorter cylinder. The amount of popcorn that filled the taller cylinder will not fill the shorter one.)

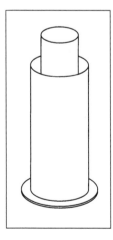

Fig. 2.15. Taller cylinder inside a shorter one

Similar Figures

The next set of problems explores the length, area, and volume of similar figures. These explorations help students develop an understanding of similarity and apply this knowledge to solve interesting problems.

Similar figures have the same shape but not necessarily the same perimeter and area. Problem 14, below, will explore the relationship between the perimeters and areas of two similar figures.

Problem 14: Similar Shapes

(Adapted from *Measurement in the Middle Grades,* activity 20, pp. 56–57, 70 [Geddes et al. 1994])

- Enlarge figure A by doubling each side to create similar figure B.

- Enlarge figure A by tripling each side to create similar figure C.

- Enlarge figure A by quadrupling each side to create similar figure D.

- Record the perimeter and area of each figure in a table like the one immediately below.

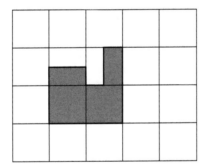

Fig A

Figure	Length of the Base	Perimeter	Area
A	2		
B			
C			
D			

- Look for patterns in the table. What can you say about the relationship between the relative lengths of the two similar figures' sides and their relative perimeters and areas?

- If the length of the base of figure A is multiplied by 5, what are the new figure's perimeter and area?

- If the perimeter of a new similar figure is 64 centimeters, what is the length of the new figure's base? What is its area?

- If the area of a new figure is 300 square cm, what is the length of the new figure's base?

- Compare the corresponding angles of two similar figures.

Materials

☑ Blackline master 2.8

Solutions to Problem 14

Figure	Length of the Base	Perimeter	Area
A	2	9	3
B	4	18	12
C	6	27	27
D	8	36	48
	16	72	192
	20	90	300

- See the Teacher's Notes below for a discussion on the relationship between the side lengths and the perimeter and area in two similar figures.

- Corresponding angles between two similar figures are congruent. In this situation all the angles are right angles.

Teacher's Notes

You can use this problem to introduce similar figures. Students can do this problem without much previous experience with similar figures. You might, however, help students by starting with an informal discussion of what the term *similar* means. You could demonstrate similarity with a square, showing how to enlarge it on a grid by doubling it both horizontally and vertically. Then enlarge the original square by doubling only it *only* horizontally *or* vertically, and not both. Ask if the resulting figure is similar to the first. (The second figure is not a square, so it is not similar to the original square.) Two figures are similar if the ratio between two corresponding side lengths is equal and corresponding angles are congruent. (See the extensions below.) The ratio of corresponding side lengths between any two similar figures is the *scale factor* between the two figures. (See the extensions below.)

Since all the angles are right angles in this activity, corresponding angles are not an immediate concern. To demonstrate the importance of angles, draw a rectangle and parallelogram with the same length sides but different corresponding angles.

After students have completed creating the similar figures, discuss the patterns that the students noticed about the similar figures. Test their conjectures with a new figure, such as a rectangle or triangle. The following are some patterns that students may observe.

> The number by which one multiplies each side in a given figure, A, to form another figure, B, is called a *scale factor*. The scale factor from A to B is 2, whereas the scale factor from A to C is 3. You could ask students to draw a figure whose side lengths are each half the side lengths of figure A. The scale factor from A to this new figure is 1/2. The scale factor from B to A is 1/2. Are the figures A and C similar? Why? The scale factor from C to A is 1/3. What is the scale factor from A to C? Are figures A and C similar? Why? When discussing the scale factor, it is important that students see that the scale factor is different if we ask between A and C and between C and A, respectively.

In this set of figures, the angles are all right angles, so the angles are congruent. Repeating this activity with a triangle might be interesting. In this situation, be sure to compare side lengths and angles. Corresponding angles are congruent, and the ratio of any two sides of one triangle is equal to the ratio of corresponding sides in the second triangle. In similar figures, corresponding angles are congruent and the ratio of corresponding side lengths in each figure is the same.

Extensions

- What are ratios of the corresponding side lengths between figures A and B? Figures A and C? Figures A and D? Explain what these numbers mean. (This ratio is 2, 3, and 4 respectively, the scale factors between figure A and figures B, C, and D.)

- Pick two sides in figure A. Find the ratio of the two sides. Find the ratio of the sides that correspond to these to sides in figures B and C. What patterns do you observe? (The ratio of side lengths in a figure is the same ratio of corresponding side lengths in a similar figure.)

- Repeat this process with another shape. Are your patterns still valid?

- Repeat this activity with a parallelogram. Compare corresponding

---

Common Core Mathematical Practices
When students explore relationships among similar figures, make conjectures about the patterns they observe, and then apply their conjectures to seek specific information, they learn to **model with mathematics.**

Common Core
Mathematical
Practices
When students extend
their understanding
of similarity to
explore whether their
conjectures apply to
a new set of figures,
they learn to **construct
viable arguments and
critique the reasoning
of others.**

angles, lengths, perimeters, and area. Do your patterns for the similar figures in this activity apply to parallelograms? Explain.

Problem 15: Building Staircases

(Adapted from *Measurement in the Middle Grades,* activity 20B, pp. 56–57, 70 [Geddes et al. 1994])

- Build a staircase like staircase A (see diagram) using identical cubes.

- Build staircase B so that each dimension is exactly twice as large as the corresponding dimensions of staircase A.

- Build staircase C so that each dimension is exactly three times as large as the corresponding dimensions of staircase A.

- Build staircase D so that each dimension is exactly four times as large as the corresponding dimensions of staircase A.

Staircases B, C, and D are similar to staircase A.

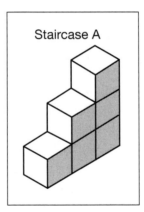

Staircase A

- Record the height, surface area, and volume of each staircase in a table.

Staircase	Height	Surface Area	Volume
A	3 units		
B			
C			
D			

- Compare the height, surface area, and volume of staircase A with those of staircase B.

- Compare the height, surface area, and volume of staircase A with those of staircase C.

- Compare the surface area and volume of staircase A with those of resulting staircase D.

- If the volume of a new figure similar to figure A is 3000 cubic units, what is the height of the new of the new figure? What is its surface area?

- If the surface area of a new figure is 350 square units, what is the height of the new figure?

Materials

☑ Blackline master 2.9—one copy for each student, unit cubes

Solutions to Problem 15

Staircase	Height	Surface Area	Volume
A	3	24	6
B	6	96	48
C	9	216	162
D	12	384	384

- If the height doubles, the surface area increases by a factor of 2 × 2, or 4, and the volume increases by a factor of 2 × 2 × 2, or 8.

- If the height triples, the surface area increases by a factor of 3 × 3, or 9, and the volume increases by a factor of 3 × 3 × 3, or 27.

- If the height increases by a factor of 4, the surface area increases by a factor of 4 × 4, or 16, and the volume increases by a factor of 4 × 4 × 4, or 64.

- If the volume is 3000 cubic units, then the height is 20 units and the surface area is 1400 square units.

- If the surface area is 350 square units, then the height is 10 units.

Teacher's Notes

This problem extends similarity to three-dimensional figures. The figures created in this activity are similar three-dimensional figures. These similar figures have the same general patterns as those found for similar two-dimensional figures in problem 14. The new feature is volume. If two figures, A and B, are similar and the scale factor from A to B is 2, then the volume of B is $2 \times 2 \times 2$, or 8, times the volume of A. In general, if two three-dimensional figures A and B are similar and the scale factor from A to B is n, then the lengths in B are n times those in A, the surface area of B is n^2 times that of A, and the volume of B is n^3 times that of A.

If students have done problem 14, this problem should be a natural springboard from two-dimensional, similar figures to three-dimensional figures. You could start with a simple rectangular prism made from two blocks, using the questions above to explore similar rectangular prisms. You can then move to the figures in problem 15.

Part 2: Visualizing and Representing Shapes

The following problems develop students' ability to visualize, represent, and interpret three-dimensional figures represented in a two-dimensional scheme. Problem 16 explores the representation of three-dimensional figures made from unit cubes on isometric dot paper. Isometric dot paper is dot paper in which the distances from a dot to each of six surrounding dots are all equivalent. Problem 17 introduces another representational plan, using a set of three two-dimensional diagrams—front view, right view, and base view—to represent a three-dimensional figure.

Problem 16: Exploring Cubes

(Adapted from *Geometry in the Middle Grades*, activity 1, pp. 20–21 [Geddes et al. 1992])

- Make a sketch of a cube on isometric dot paper. Describe how your sketch represents the properties of a cube. Compare your sketch with those of your classmates. Are they the same? Explain.

- Make a rectangular prism with three cubes. Make a sketch of the rectangular prism on isometric dot paper. How many different ways can you represent the prism on the dot paper?

Materials

☑ Identical unit cubes, blackline master 2.4 and blackline master 2.1—one copy of each per student

Solutions to Problem 16

- You can draw two isometric views of a cube:

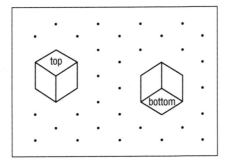

The parallelograms on the isometric dot paper represent the square faces of a cube. The edges are line segments with the same length. Only three of the cube's six faces are visible.

- You can draw six isometric views of a rectangular prism made from three unit cubes:

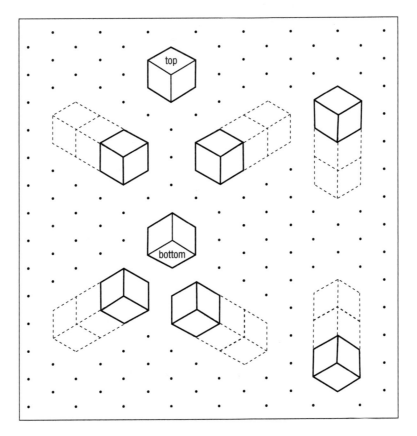

Teacher's Notes

This problem helps students develop the skills necessary to represent three-dimensional figures on a two-dimensional plane. Start by asking students about special features of a cube. Concepts such as *vertex, point, line, edge, parallel* and *perpendicular lines, skew lines, plane, angle, right angle, parallel* and *perpendicular planes, rectangle, diagonal,* and so on, naturally arise in students' discussion about the cube and its representation on isometric dot paper.

Students can draw two views of a cube on isometric dot paper, one showing the cube's top face and one showing its bottom face. To create these two views, sketch two squares on the isometric dot paper. (They will look like diamonds or parallelograms on the dot paper.) On one of the squares, draw the edges up and complete the cube. This drawing will show a cube whose bottom face is visible. On the other square, draw the edges down and complete the cube. This drawing will show a cube whose top face is visible. You can shade the bottom and top on each cube to focus the visualization. Students may have other ways to draw the cube. For example, some may start with a Y-shaped figure and complete the cube. Another strategy is to draw a hexagon and then draw line segments in the interior to complete the figure to represent a cube (see fig. 2.16).

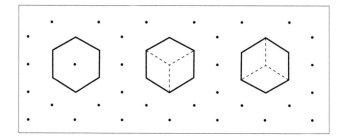

Fig. 2.16. Drawing a cube on isometric dot paper by starting with a hexagon

Let students discuss the features of a cube or rectangular prism that are preserved or not preserved on an isometric representation.

Extensions

- Sketch several isometric views of an L-shaped figure made with four cubes (see fig. 2.17).

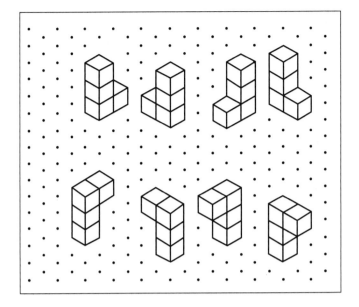

Fig. 2.17. L-shaped figures, made with four cubes, depicted on isometric dot paper

- A flat pattern or network made up of five squares is called a *pentomino*. You can fold it to form an open box. Sketch several pentominoes on square grid paper. How many different pentominoes are possible? (Twelve different representations are possible; see fig. 2.18.)

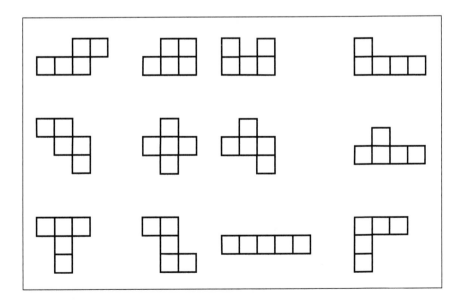

Fig. 2.18. The twelve possible representations of a pentomino

- Which pentomino has the least perimeter? The greatest?

- A hexomino is a flat, six-square pattern that you can fold to make a closed box or cube. Sketch several hexominoes on grid paper.

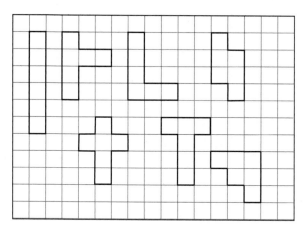

Problem 17: Representing Buildings Made from Cubes

(Adapted from *Geometry in the Middle Grades,* activity 1, p. 21 [Geddes et al. 1992])

Models of buildings are frequently created by using cubes and represented by the front, side, and bottom (or top) views of the model. To explore this representation you will need a building mat that is a blank sheet of paper labeled "Front," "Back," "Left," and "Right" as shown in figure 2.19.

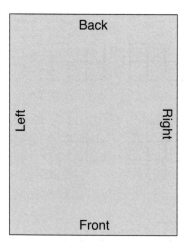

Fig. 2.19. Building mat created by labeling a blank sheet of paper as shown

Another important piece of information in building and representing buildings is a *base plan,* which is a drawing of the base of the building with the numbers on the squares indicating how high each stack of cubes is. For example, see the following base plan:

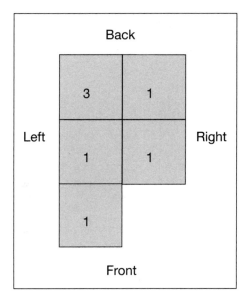

- On a building mat, build the building represented in the base plan shown. How many cubes do you need to build the bottom layer? How many cubes do you need to build the building?

- Turn the building mat so that you can look at the front, back, left, and right views of the building. Match each view with one of the views below:

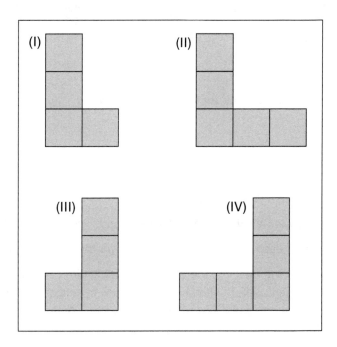

Which view is the view from the front side? Back? Right? Left?

- What do you observe about the four views?

Build the following building on your mat plan.

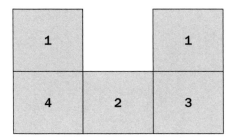

Floor Plan

View the building from the front, back, right, and left sides. Which view of the building does each view represent? Use these views to sketch the other three views.

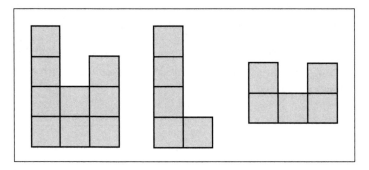

Materials

☑ Blackline master 2.10—one copy for each student

☑ Unit cubes

Solutions to Problem 17

- Five cubes are in the first layer. The building has a total of seven cubes.

- View I is the front view. View II is the left view. View III is the back view, and view IV is the right view.

- The front and back views are reflections of each other. The same is true for the left and right views.

- The first representation is the front view of the building; the second, the right view; and the third, the base view. You can use the first representation to sketch the back view by reflecting the representation over a vertical line. A similar process with the right view will create the left view.

Teacher's Notes

This problem shows another way to build and represent three-dimensional buildings. This representational scheme is similar to one that architects use, except they use a top view rather than a base plan.

In discussing the first building, students should notice that the left and right sides are mirror images, or *reflections*, of each other, and that the front and back are also reflections of each other. Thus, given the front view, one can quickly draw the back view. The same is true for the right and left sides. You might want to have students practice drawing mirror images of each side.

Extensions

- Use unit cubes to build the following building. Draw the base-, front-, and right-side views of the building.

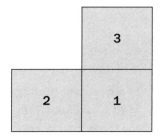

- Use the following set of building plans and unit cubes to construct a building.

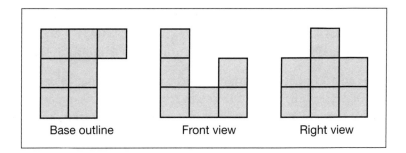

Base outline   Front view   Right view

Common Core Mathematical Practices

When students move back and forth between three-dimensional objects and a two-dimensional representation of the objects, noting salient features that the representation does or does not preserve, they learn to **use appropriate tools strategically** and **look for and express regularity in repeated reasoning.**

Problem 18: Parallelogram and Triangular Grids

(Adapted from *Geometry in the Middle Grades,* activities 8B and 8C, pp. 50–51 [Geddes et al. 1992])

- We have formed the grid in figure 2.20 by sets of parallel lines. What shapes do you see in the grid? Are any of the shapes similar? Explain.

If a pair of figures is similar, how do the corresponding side lengths and area compare?

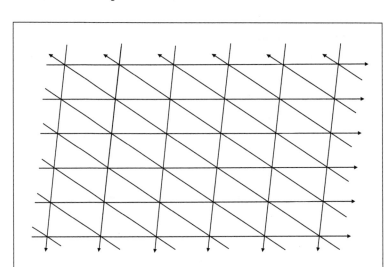

Fig. 2.20. A grid formed by sets of parallel lines

- Outline a triangle that has a line joining the midpoints of two of its sides. This line is called a *midline*. Compare the length of the midline with the length of the third side. What do you notice? Explain why this relationship exists. Repeat your conjecture for another triangle. Does your conjecture still hold?

- Label three angles of a triangle as *A*, *C*, and *T*. Choose three different colors. With the first color, color in the angle *C* and all the angles near points *C*, *A*, and *T* that are congruent to angle *C*. Repeat this process with the two other colors chosen for angles *A* and *T*. What do you observe about the angles around *C*? Around *A*? Around *T*?

- Find a straight angle in the colored diagram. What colors are in the angles that make up the straight angle? Repeat this process for two more straight angles. What conjecture can you make about the angle sum of triangle *CAT*?

Materials

☑ Blackline master 2.11—one copy for each student

Solutions to Problem 18

- One can find differently shaped parallelograms, equilateral triangles, trapezoids, and hexagons on the grid. Each of those shapes has similar shapes on the grid. The ratio of corresponding side lengths is the same for each pair of corresponding side lengths in the two similar figures. This number is called the *scale factor*. The area of one similar figure is the scale factor times the scale factor of the other area. That is, the areas of two similar figures are to each other as the squares of the corresponding sides.

- The line joining the midpoints of two sides of a triangle is parallel to the third side and has a length equal to one-half the length of the third side.

- The sum of the measures of the angles of a triangle is equal to the measure of a straight angle (180 degrees).

Teacher's Notes

This activity provides an opportunity to explore shapes, similarity, angle sum of a triangle, and midpoint lines. In addition, questions about parallel lines can be raised, for example, the relationship between corresponding angles, between alternating interior angles, and so on. This exploration allows students to visualize relationships and make many different conjectures. Encourage students to explain why their conjectures are true.

Extensions

- Form an exterior angle of a triangle from one side of the triangle and the extension of an adjacent side. Going counterclockwise, form the triangle's three exterior angles. Explore the sum of these three angles. (The sum is always 360 degrees, even if one proceeds clockwise instead.)

Common Core Mathematical Practices
When students look for patterns, make conjectures, and validate their claims, they learn to **construct viable arguments and critique the reasoning of others.**

Problem 19: Slides, Flips, and Turns

(Adapted from *Geometry in the Middle Grades,* activity 16, pp. 63–64, 68–69 [Geddes et al. 1992])

You can move figures about a plane by transformations. The pictures below show figures transformed by a slide, reflection, and rotation.

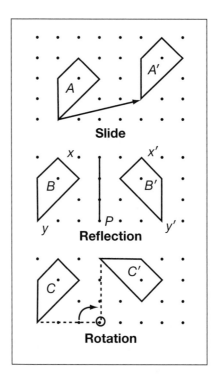

Figure *A′* is the slide image of figure *A*. The slide arrow shows the direction of the slide. In this example, by using the dot paper we can say the direction is 4 to the right and 1 up.

Figure *B′* is the reflection image of figure *B* about line *p*. Notice that the reflection line is the perpendicular bisector of a line segment joining a point on the original figure to its corresponding point on the image.

Figure *C′* is the image of figure *C* under a rotation around the point *O*. The rotation or turn is indicated by the size of the angle. The angle has a point as its vertex and sides that connect two corresponding points on the similar figures to *O*.

Use the activity sheet for this problem to answer the following questions.

- Which figures are slide images of figure *A*? Indicate the slide arrow.

- Which figures are reflection images of figure *A*? Find the flip line.

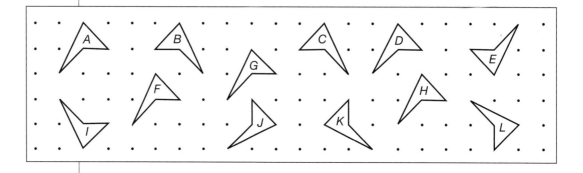

- Draw each reflection image using the dotted line as the reflection line.

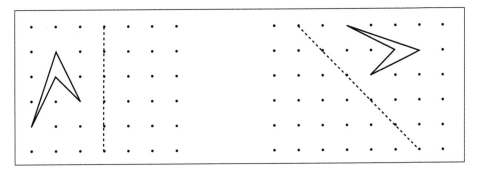

- Rotate figure *CAT* 180 degrees around point *O*. Check your result by using tracing paper (trace figure *CAT*, and turn the tracing paper copy to see if fits on top of your answer).

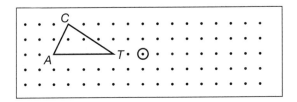

- Describe one motion that will map the first figure onto the second.

  Map figure *A* onto figure *B*.

  Map figure *A* onto figure *C*.

  Map figure *B* onto figure *D*.

  Map figure *B* onto figure *E*.

  Map figure *E* onto figure *C*.

  Map figure *C* onto figure *E*.

  Map figure *A* onto figure *F*.

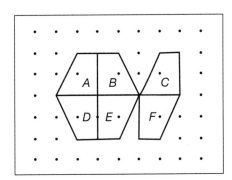

- Examine what occurs if you reflect a figure over two parallel lines. That is, reflect figure *A* over line *c* to form image *A'*, then reflect image *A'* over line *d* to form image *A''*. How is figure *A* related to image *A''*? Is it possible to get from figure *A* to image *A''* in one motion? Describe.

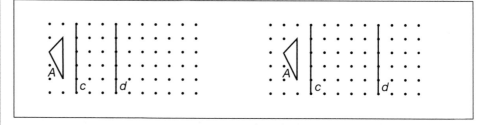

- Repeat the previous problem, but this time do two reflections over intersecting lines.

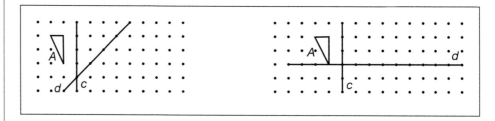

What prediction might you make about the results obtained by doing two reflections over intersecting lines?

Materials

☑ Blackline master 2.12, blackline master 2.1, tracing paper.

Solutions to Problem 19

- Figures *D, G, F,* and *H* are slide images of figure *A*.
- Reflection images using the dotted line as the reflection line:

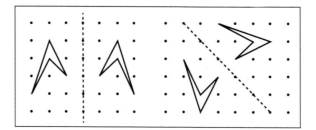

- Rotating figure *CAT* 180 degrees around point *O*:

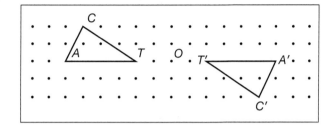

- Map figure *A* onto figure *B*. This mapping can be done with a reflection.

  Map figure *A* onto figure *C*. This mapping can be done with a slide.

  Map figure *B* onto figure *D*. This mapping can be done with a reflection.

  Map figure *B* onto figure *E*. This mapping can be done with a reflection.

  Map figure *E* onto figure *C*. This mapping can be done with a rotation.

  Map figure *C* onto figure *E*. This mapping can be done with a rotation.

  Map figure *A* onto figure *F*. This mapping can be done with a rotation.

- Reflecting a figure over two parallel lines:

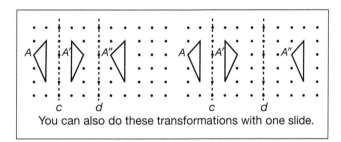

You can also do these transformations with one slide.

- Two reflections of the figure over intersecting lines:

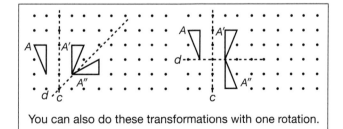

You can also do these transformations with one rotation.

Common Core Mathematical Practices

When students explore properties of figures that are preserved under transformations, they learn to **look for and express regularity in repeated reasoning** and **model with mathematics.**

Teacher's Notes

The goal of this problem is to introduce students to slides (translations), flips (reflections), and turns (rotations). Rotations are the most difficult for students to visualize. Transparent paper is a useful tool to help with the visualization. NCTM Illuminations (http://illuminations.nctm.org) also has some nice applets that can enhance the process of performing the transformations.

Discussing and questioning students' results should lead to a consideration of what properties are preserved under slides, reflections, and rotations. Each of the three transformations is an *isometry*—that is, the resulting figure is congruent to the original figure. Orientation is not preserved under a reflection.

You can start the problem by demonstrating a reflection. Students can then draw reflections and explore the relationship between the two figures and the reflection line. Repeat this process for each of the other two transformations.

REFERENCES

Geddes, Dorothy, with Juliana Bove, Irene Fortunato, David J. Fuys, Jessica Morgenstern, and Rosamond Welchman-Tischler. *Geometry in the Middle Grades. Curriculum and Evaluation Standards for School Mathematics* Addenda Series, Grades 5–8. Reston, Va.: National Council of Teachers of Mathematics, 1992.

Geddes, Dorothy, with Robert Berkman, Iris Fearon, Michael Fishenfeld, Caroline Forlano, David J. Fuys, Jodi Goldstein, and Rosamond Welchman. *Measurement in the Middle Grades. Curriculum and Evaluation Standards for School Mathematics* Addenda Series, Grades 5–8. Reston, Va.: National Council of Teachers of Mathematics, 1994.

Data and Chance

PROBLEMS and activities involving data and chance in middle school mathematics need to build on students' natural use of the ideas and understandings that they develop from their daily experiences. Dealing with data and chance provides opportunities to capture core ideas of the middle school curriculum—proportional reasoning and generalization. The fundamental mathematical concepts that underlie statistics and probability are grounded in proportional reasoning. We selected this chapter's problems to nudge students toward using their solutions in general situations that are similar to, but at least slightly different from, the ones encountered in the problems.

In problem 1, Is This Game Fair?, students analyze games from a probabilistic perspective to determine whether the players have evenly distributed chances of winning. This experience uses proportional reasoning in applying probability and statistics. The processes of analyzing the games and creating others require students to generalize their ideas to new, although similar, situations.

Problem 2, Monte Carlo Simulation, features simulations that require students to create a procedure that can model changing situations, and it thus requires notions of generalization. The problem embeds proportional reasoning throughout as students use probability to represent the relationships among various aspects of the modeled situation.

Problem 3, A Look at Average Wage, uses a manufacturing and marketing company as a context in which to consider the notion of "average" from different points of view. The purposes are (1) to show how selecting the mean, median, or mode to represent central tendency may result in different answers to the same question; and (2), to use that phenomenon to consider the foundational concepts of each measure of central tendency.

The fourth problem, Light-Bulb Life, focuses on using standard deviation to compare distributions.

In Family Combinations of Boys and Girls, students model all the possible boy-girl combinations that can make up five-child families and identify each one's probability. This problem serves as a specific example of listing all possible events and then considering each particular, described event's probability therein.

In the final problem, Montana Red Dog, students learn a card game that depends on analyzing the probability of beating the dealer's card. After learning to play the game, you can ask specific questions about the various events' probability.

Each problem embeds students' learning of statistics and probability ideas in a realistic context to help students realize the various concepts' depth of application and how to generalize those ideas to other situations.

Problem 1: Is This Game Fair?

(Adapted from *Dealing with Data and Chance,* illustration 3, pp. 12–14, 61–62, by Hope Martin [Zawojewski et al. 1991])

- Find a partner to play Sum of Seven (blackline master 3.1).

- Decide who is the player and who is the opponent.

- The player and opponent each start with ten points.

- Each time the player rolls a sum of 7, the opponent must transfer three points to the player.

- Each time the player rolls a sum *other* than 7, she or he must transfer one point to the opponent.

- Record the result of each roll on the score sheet (blackline master 3.1).

- The participant with the most points at the end of ten rolls is the winner.

- A participant who runs out of points before the end of the ten rolls automatically loses.

Investigate: Is this game fair? (Use blackline master 3.1.)
Analyze: Is this game fair? (Use blackline master 3.2.)
How can you make the game fair?

Materials

☑ One pair of six-sided number cubes for each pair of students (each numbered 1 through 6)

☑ Blackline master 3.1 (one copy for each student)

☑ Calculators

☑ Blackline master 3.2 (one overhead transparency)

Teacher's Notes

Is This Game Fair? will use statistical reasoning to detect a potentially unfair game, employ probabilistic reasoning to determine whether the game is fair, and then if it isn't, use probabilistic reasoning to modify the game to make it fair.

Begin by handing out copies of blackline master 3.1 to students and having students play the game. Once they learn the gist of the game from the activity sheet, have them to play the game at least ten times. When questions about the game's fairness begin to emerge, ask students to raise their hands indicating whether the game seems fair or unfair. Have students write reasons for their fair-or-unfair decision independently on a piece of paper or in their mathematics journals. Then ask a few students to share what they have written.

Direct each pair of students to report the numbers of player's wins and opponent's wins, Record the tally on the chalkboard, showing the results across the whole class. Direct each pair to calculate the percents of games won by the player and by the opponent, first for their own set of games played and then for the whole class. Pose the following questions for discussion: "Now that you have these data, do you feel more or less strongly about your fair-or-unfair decision? Why?" If the data are not yet convincing, have the students play a few more rounds of the game, revise their data, and report new percents for the tally chart. Repeat this process until the data tell the story.

Once the opponent's advantage in this game becomes clear from the data, guide the students through formally analyzing the probabilities for rolling and not rolling a sum of 7. Use the overhead transparency of blackline master 3.2 to display each sum for every combination from rolling the two number cubes. Once you have filled the table in, ask the following questions:

- What is the probability for rolling a sum of 7?

- What is the probability for rolling a sum that is *not* 7?

- What are the odds in favor of rolling a sum of 7?

- What are the odds against rolling a sum of 7?

  Modify the game so that it is fair for both players. (At this point, have students work in pairs. Analyze the fairness of each modification that each pair poses, using the filled-in blackline master 3.2 transparency.)

Note that probability is a *measure* of chance. Before students deal with the formal mathematics of probability, they need to understand the meaning of chance and have some experience naturally quantifying the concept of likelihood. This problem offers students an opportunity to explore the concept of equally likely chances and describe chance quantitatively. For example, when students say, "The opponent is more likely to win" or "The player's chances of winning are not as good as the opponent's," they are intuitively comparing the chances of winning—the first step in quantifying chance.

Common Core Mathematical Practices
When students use statistical reasoning to detect a potentially unfair game, and then use probabilistic reasoning to determine the fairness and to modify an unfair game, they *reason abstractly and quantitatively.* Further, having students modify the game to make it fair requires them to *make sense of the problem and persevere in solving it.*

Solution to Problem 1

Is This Game Fair? Transparency: Blackline Master 3.2

		Die No. 1					
	+	**1**	**2**	**3**	**4**	**5**	**6**
	1	2	3	4	5	6	7
	2	3	4	5	6	7	8
Die No. 2	**3**	4	5	6	7	8	9
	4	5	6	7	8	9	10
	5	6	7	8	9	10	11
	6	7	8	9	10	11	12

P(sum of 7) = $^6/_{36}$, or $^1/_6$.

P(not a sum of 7) = $^{30}/_{36}$, or $^5/_6$.

Odds (sum of 7) = 1 to 5.

Odds (not a sum of 7) = 4 to 5.

You can modify the game a number of ways to make it fair. One is to consider the odds in favor of rolling a 7 as a means to determine the number of points transferred on each turn. In particular, if the player rolls a 7, the opponent should transfer five points to the player instead of the three points that the game's starting rules indicate.

Extensions

- Teams can play the game again with a new five-point rule. Gather data to verify that this rule does, indeed, make the game fair.

- Play the same game, but when the player rolls a double, the opponent gives up three points to the player; and when the player rolls anything other than a double, the player gives up one point to the opponent. Ask for students' opinions about whether this game is fair, and have them gather data to support or refute their opinions. Then analyze the game as you did for Sum of Seven. (This game is essentially the same as the original one, because the odds in favor of rolling a double are 1 to 5.)

Problem 2: Monte Carlo Simulation

(Adapted from *Dealing with Data and Chance,* illustration 4, pp. 14–16, by Marsha Landau [Zawojewski et al. 1991])

Design a Monte Carlo simulation to solve the following problem:

> The Tripl-Bubl Gum Company decided to promote its gum by including in each pack the photograph of one of six rock-music stars. Assuming that the company will issue equal numbers of photographs of each of the six stars and that, when you buy a pack of gum, your chances of getting any of the six photographs are the same, about how many packs of gum would you expect to have to buy to get all six photographs? (Adapted from Travers and Gray [1981, p. 327])

Materials

- ☑ Six slips of paper
- ☑ A hat
- ☑ Number cubes
- ☑ Six-section spinners (or another random-number device, such as a computer-based, random-number generator)
- ☑ Calculators

Teacher's Notes

This problem engages students in using probability to model a realistic situation mathematically. Simulations are important for exploring solutions to problems that are impossible, too dangerous, or too expensive to carry out in a conventional experiment. The Monte Carlo method of simulation uses random-number devices, such as dice, number cubes, coins, spinners, or computer-generated random numbers, to represent the mathematical characteristics of a real-world situation. The theoretical basis for the Monte Carlo simulation method is the law of large numbers: as you run a simulation more and more times, the simulated estimate (see below) for the probability more and more closely approximates the theoretical probability (Watkins 1981). You design a model of the situation, conduct experiments in the simulated setting to generate data, and then analyze that data as though they were real.

$$\text{Simulated Estimate} = \frac{\text{Number of Successes}}{\text{Number of Trials}}$$

Common Core Mathematical Practices

When students develop a simulation to represent the situation in this problem, they *model with mathematics.* As part of the modeling process, students interpret the simulation's results in the context of the rock-star-card collection, reflect on whether the simulation's results make sense, and possibly revise their simulation to represent the situation better.

This activity is an "expected value" problem that middle school students find interesting but cannot solve analytically. The problem's setting also is too expensive and inconvenient to experiment with directly in the real world. For expected-value problems, you use the simulated data to estimate the "expected value" of real data by calculating the following ratio:

$$\frac{\text{Sum of Results from All Individual Trials}}{\text{Number of Trials}}$$

After students have read the problem, give them the following questions to discuss:

- About how many packs of gum would you expect to have to buy? (Answers will vary from 6 to n.)

- Is it possible to get all six photographs by buying only six packs of gum? Is this likely to happen? (Yes; very unlikely.)

- Is it possible *not* to get all six photographs if buying 100 packs of gum? Is this likely to happen? (Yes; very unlikely.)

- Has anyone had an experience of collecting objects in offers like the one described? (Answers will vary.)

Tell students that to solve the problem, they will need to think about ways to act out the situation using materials available in the classroom. Ask them to consider first the situation's following essential mathematical characteristics:

- Each pack of gum contains one of six rock-music-star photographs.

- A particular pack of gum has one chance in six of containing any particular photograph.

- Duplicates are possible.

Ask the following question:

- What could we use in place of packs of gum to represent the problem situation?

One example would be to put six slips of paper, numbered 1, 2, 3, 4, 5, and 6, into a container and draw one out to represent each purchase of a pack of gum. You would then return the piece of paper to the container and run a new trial. The goal is to determine how many trials you would need to obtain a full set of the numbers 1 through 6 (i.e., to represent the full set of photographs). The simulation is most fun when each pair of students has several random-number devices available to choose from. Before starting to run the experiments, discuss how each random-number device provides six different outcomes, with each outcome being equally likely and with duplicates being possible.

Tell students to work in pairs to run at least four experiments. On the chalkboard, draw a sample tally chart like the one below for students to use in gathering their data. Tell the pairs of students to be prepared to report to the whole class, "For each experiment, how many packs of gum did you have to buy before obtaining a complete set of rock-star photographs?" (You may need to remind students to stop once they have drawn all six rock-star photographs.)

Sample Tally Chart

	Exp. 1	Exp. 2	Exp. 3
Rock Star 1	//	//	///// /
Rock Star 2	/////	//	//
Rock Star 3	/	/////	/////
Rock Star 4	///	/	////
Rock Star 5	//	/	/
Rock Star 6	////	//	///
Total No. of Packs of Gum	17	13	21

Once each pair of students has run at least four experiments, stop the work and ask each pair to report the number of packs of gum for each experiment completed. Write each of the sixty or so data points on the chalkboard as a frequency distribution (i.e., write the numbers in order in a column from the top of the chalkboard to the bottom, and write repeats of any numbers next to one another to the right of the original number.) Have the class determine the range, the median, and the mode. Then ask the pairs to calculate the mean, which should be around 15. Discuss how the mean, median, and mode compare. Then come to consensus as a class on how many packs of gum a person should expect to buy to obtain the full set of rock-star photographs. You could describe this number as a narrow range or an estimated value. Discuss whether buying this much gum to obtain the full set of photographs would be "worth it." (The expected number of packs of gum is about fifteen. To see the calculation of the theoretical expected value, which is 14.7 packs of gum, see Lappan and Winter [1980], p. 448.)

Extensions

- Discuss ways to improve the simulated estimate. Running more trials would tap the law of large numbers and thereby improve the estimate.

- Discuss whether the results were, and should be, different when using different random-number devices. For example, many children hold down a corner of the spinner and thereby alter the "fairness" of the device; some dice may be physically altered (a chip off a corner) and therefore not be perfectly balanced; and so on.

- Ask students how they would need to modify the simulation to represent a collection of eight rock-star photographs.

- Pose a new problem: The Kid has challenged the Doc to a pie-throwing contest. Both have bad aims. The probability that Doc hits the Kid on any one throw is $^1/_{10}$, and the probability that the Kid hits Doc on any one throw is $^1/_5$. Doc really would not like to get whipped cream on the fancy tie he is wearing, so he thinks that throwing pies might be a bad idea. "Okay," says the Kid, "to even things out, you can go first, and we'll alternate throws until one of us gets hit." Doc wonders whether this suggestion really evens things out. Does it? Design a simulation to answer this question. (Adapted from Watkins [1981], p. 204)

Problem 3: A Look at Average Wage

(Adapted from *Dealing with Data and Chance*, illustration 7, pp. 27–29, 66–67, by Albert P. Shulte [Zawojewski et al. 1991])

Blackline master 3.3 depicts a situation that reveals different interpretations for a set of data, each using a different measure of central tendency. The setting is an industrial company in which a union official and the company president are discussing the possibility of increasing company employees' wages. Using different central tendency measures, each interprets the current average wage situation differently, setting the stage for students to learn about mean, median, and mode through a real-life problem.

Materials

☑ Blackline master 3.3

☑ Calculators

☑ Computer and spreadsheet software (optional, for the extension)

Teacher's Notes

This problem will introduce students to mean, median, and mode by asking them to interpret each in the context of a realistic situation. One commonly teaches measures of central tendency (i.e., mean, median, and mode) by defining them and then applying the definitions to small sets of numbers. A more effective method of introducing the three measures is in a more complex, decision-making, problem-solving environment. This problem assumes that students have learned how to find the arithmetic average, or mean, but you can use it to introduce median and mode.

Distribute copies of both pages of blackline master 3.3, A Look at Average Wage, to each student. Have students read the story on blackline master 3.3's first page aloud. Pause when the story introduces the terms *mode* and *median,* and ask questions to ensure that each student understands what these two measures mean. Use question 1 on blackline master 3.3's second page to review one way the company could distribute pay raises. Then pose the following questions:

Solutions to Problem 3

New median: $30,000

New mode: $30,000

New mean: $47,250

What salary position do you support? (Answers will vary. Students should support their positions with explicit statements of assumptions about how they made their judgments.)

- Which measures of central tendency stayed the same? (Median and mode)

- Which measures of central tendency changed? (Mean) Why? (Because the greater amounts paid to those with the lower salaries increased the mean salary paid across all individuals. However, this change did not affect the median and mode, because they are single data points in the data set. Changes in data extremes thus affect median and mode infrequently, whereas they *always* affect the mean.)

- If you changed only one or two salaries, which measure of central tendency would surely change? (The mean would surely change, because its calculation includes *all* values.)

- If you changed only one or two salaries, which measure of central tendency would be most likely to stay the same? (The mode is mostly likely to stay the same, because it is the most frequently occurring salary, and only one or two salaries are changing.)

- If you change only one or two salaries, how likely is the median to change? (It depends. If the median lies in the middle of several same-sized salaries, it will not change. If the median is close to a different salary level, it will more likely change.)

Common Core Mathematical Practices

When students pose and defend different salary positions to one another, they *construct viable arguments and critique the reasoning of others.*

Use question 2 on the second page of blackline master 3.3 to initiate a discussion based on conclusions drawn from data summarized in the table on the same blackline master page. Have small groups of students develop position statements and report to class. The discussion question can have a number of reasonable answers. Management would naturally favor focusing on the mean because it keeps the management salaries high, whereas the union leader would prefer to focus on the median, the number of lower-paid employees, and the mode, because the workers' salaries would be improved. Students may also consider the fact that the company may have only a certain number of dollars available to be distributed across all employees. Teachers can promote students' consideration of multiple solutions by having them write up or present two reasonable alternatives, and to be explicit about their rationale for each alternative. At first, students may simply take ideas from one another without much reflection. As the school year progresses and the teacher continues to value creative, reasonable alternatives, however, students will begin to enjoy actively looking for reasonable, alternative solutions.

Extensions

- Have students enter the employees' salaries into a computer spreadsheet. Column A could list the number of employees by type, and column B could list the salary of that type. Display the mean salary for all employees at the bottom of the spreadsheet in a cell labeled "Mean Salary." (Define the cell as the total salary value divided by the total number of employees.) Use the spreadsheet to display the new salaries, and calculate the new mean for each of the following situations.

  1. Use the spreadsheet to predict the mean if the salaries of the lowest-paid employees increased to $30,000.

  2. Use the spreadsheet to investigate how much of a raise the president would have to give himself to raise the mean average wage in the company by $1000.

  3. The company has hired two new employees—a plant manager and a foreman. Predict whether the mean salary will increase, decrease, or stay the same. Explain your prediction. Check your prediction by using the spreadsheet.

- Students and the teacher should bring in newspaper articles and other sources of real-world data summaries. Often such sources report the median instead of the mean, especially when extreme values occur in the data sets. For example, sources in the United States usually express housing costs as medians, because a small number of extremely expensive homes raises the mean to a point at which many consider that this "average" inflates the impression of home costs. Thus, U.S. data sources usually use the median to represent the central tendency of home costs.

Problem 4: Light-Bulb Life

(Adapted from *Dealing with Data and Chance,* illustration 8, pp. 29–32, 68–69, by Barbara Wilmot [Zawojewski et al. 1991])

Blackline master 3.4 depicts a situation in which students compare light bulbs from three different companies for the bulbs' length of life, or *longevity*. The situation introduces the notion of standard deviation as a means to compare and contrast data sets on the basis of the data's distribution. In this example, each set of bulbs has identical mean length of life, but each of the distributions, as reflected in its standard deviation, tells a very different story.

Materials

☑ Blackline master 3.4

☑ Scientific calculators

Teacher's Notes

This problem teaches early ideas related to measures of spread—in this situation, standard deviation—before we would expect students to compute standard deviations. Although the problem assumes that students have had experience finding mean, median, and range, it does not assume any knowledge of standard deviation. A prerequisite understanding needed for the problem is for students to know how to interpret stem-and-leaf plots and use the statistics function on a scientific calculator, although you can use this problem to teach the latter. Note that the calculator assumes the burden of calculating a standard deviation, whereas the problem helps students acquire an initial concept of standard deviation as a measure of data spread.

Direct students to read the narrative and stem-and-leaf plots on blackline master 3.4, and ask the following questions:

- How many tests were run for Company A? (Thirty data points indicate 30 test bulbs.)

- What is the range of bulb life for Company A? (Twenty-seven to 99 days, thus the range is 72.)

- What is the median bulb life for Company A? *(73.5 days)*

After entering the foregoing values into the table on blackline master 3.4, direct students to enter the data for Company A into their scientific calculators by using the statistics function. Have them use their calculators to find the mean and

Note about Light-Bulb Life: Using the Calculator

The calculator finds the standard deviation using a formula that involves subtracting each data point from the mean, squaring each of those differences, adding all the differences, dividing by the number of tests, and then finding the square root. Student will learn this calculation in later mathematics classes, so it is not a goal for this work.

standard deviation for the data for Company A. Then have students complete the rest of the table.

Solution to Problem 4

Summary Statistics for Each Light-Bulb Company

	No. of Tests	Range	Mean	Median	Standard Deviation
Company A	30	72 (99–27)	69.333…	73.5	22.5
Company B	30	37 (91–54)	69.333…	68.5	8.9
Company C	30	56 (93–37)	69.333…	65.5	14.3

Common Core Mathematical Practices

This introduction to standard deviation demonstrates *using appropriate tools strategically.* In this instance, the technology enables students to visualize and quantify distributions, offering them opportunities to develop an initial, deep understanding of what *standard deviation* means.

Discuss the similarities and differences among the sets of data related to the distribution of the data by asking the following questions:

- How is the shape of Company B's stem-and-leaf plot different from that of Company A? (Company A's plot is flatter and more spread out.)

- Next consider the range for Company A and Company B. How is the shape of the plot reflected in the range? (Company A's range is wider, as we can see in the height of the plot.)

- How is the shape of Company C's stem-and-leaf plot different from that of Company A? (Company A's plot seems to bulge at the top end of the times, whereas Company C's plot bulges more in the middle.)

- How does the shape of the plots for each company relate to the two medians? (The median for Company A is closer to the top of the plot, the higher times, than that for Company B, as reflected by the location of the bulges in the plots.)

Discuss what the numbers under the "standard deviation" column mean by posing the following questions:

- How do the plots and the standard deviations compare for Companies A and B? Companies A and C? Companies B and C? (The greater the range in the plot, the larger the standard deviation.)

- Which company has the largest standard deviation? (Company A)

- Which company has the smallest standard deviation? (Company B)

- How can you predict which company will have the largest and smallest standard deviation *without* looking at the numbers for standard deviation? (Looking at the plot and selecting the data that are most spread out helps identify the data set that has the largest standard deviation. Similarly, selecting the plot in which the data are least spread out helps identify the data set that has the smallest standard deviation.)

- Each company advertises the same average longevity for its bulbs. Are the companies being truthful? What are they neglecting to tell the consumer? From which company would you want to buy bulbs? Why? (Just knowing the mean length of life for the bulb does not convey the notion of bulb consistency. The desired factor of consistency likely depends on the context. For example, a custodian in a school might want bulbs with a small standard deviation, because when one bulb goes out, simply replacing all the bulbs at once may be more efficient than getting the ladder out and putting it back each time a bulb goes out. Thus, the more consistent the life of the bulbs is across bulbs, the less waste in tossing out bulbs that still work—because they probably do not have much life left in them.)

Extensions

- Suppose that these sets of data are the measurements of the diameters of ball bearings that fit into a machine. The machine works best with bearings with a diameter of 69 mm but will tolerate a difference of plus or minus 2 mm. Which company's ball bearings should be used? Why?

- Suppose that these three sets of data were salaries (in thousands) of the top executives in three companies. For which company would you rather work? Why?

- Tell students that the following rule holds for standard deviation, and pose the given situation:

  In normally distributed data, 68 percent (approximately two-thirds of the numbers) of the data points fall within one standard deviation of the mean. Have the students add and subtract one standard deviation from the means for each company. Check whether approximately two-thirds of the data points fall within this range for each company.

Problem 5: Family Combinations of Boys and Girls

(Adapted from *Patterns and Functions,* extension 2.2, pp. 29–31 [Phillips et al. 1991])

Part A: Suppose that in a certain town, Andersonville, all families have the last name of Anderson and all families have exactly five children. How many different combinations of boy-girl families would you expect to find in Andersonville?

Part B: What is the probability of having all girls in a family of five in Andersonville?

Solutions to Problem 5

Family Combinations of Boys and Girls

Part A: 32 combinations

Part B: P(all girls in families of 5 children) = $^1/_{32}$.

Teacher's Notes

This problem, adapted from Phillips et al. (1986), will introduce students to binomial probabilities, which are based on two equally likely events (e.g., heads vs. tails in a coin flip). Students will look at all the different combinations of boys and girls in families of equivalent size. The first part addresses representing the situation in an organized manner and interpreting the organization. The second part uses that representation to explore questions about probability.

To introduce students to this problem, ask, "How many of you come from a family of five children? Describe the children as a number of boys and girls, starting with the oldest. Do you think that more combinations are possible?" As an experiment, groups of students can generate families of five children by flipping a coin. Let heads be boys and tails be girls. Flip the coin five times, and write down the combinations. The first flip represents the oldest child; the second flip, the second-oldest child; and so on. For example, HTHHT produces boy, girl, boy, boy, girl. Emphasize that the order boy-girl is different from girl-boy. After the experiment, collect the data and ask, "How many groups have a family of five boys, five girls, or four boys and one girl? In how many different ways can four boys and one girl occur?" If B stands for boy and G stands for girl, the possibilities are these:

BBBBG, BBBGB, BBGBB, BGBBB, and GBBBB

Look at combinations of three boys and two girls, two boys and three girls, and one boy and four girls. Have students make a list of the possible combinations, as in the chart below.

5 Boys	4 Boys	3 Boys	2 Boys	1 Boy	0 Boys
BBBBB	BBBBG	BBBGG	BBGGG	BGGGG	GGGGG
	BBBGB	BBGBG	BGBGG	GBGGG	
	BBGBB	BGBBG	BGGBG	GGBGG	
	BGBBB	GBBBG	BGGGB	GGGBG	
	GBBBB	BBGGB	GBBGG	GGGGB	
		BGBGB	GBGBG		
		GBBGB	GBGGB		
		BGGBB	GGBBG		
		GBGBB	GGBGB		
		GGBBB	GGGBB		
1	5	10	10	5	1

Ask the following questions:

- How many different combinations of children are possible? (32)
- How many families have at least one girl? (31)
- At least two girls? (26)
- At most three boys? (26)

Have students make up their own questions to ask one another about the families. Some questions they may pose are the following:

- How many families have boys as the first two children? (8)
- How many families have a girl as the last child? (16)
- How many families have exactly three girls? (10)
- How many families have a boy as the third child? (16)
- How many families have a boy and a girl for the first two children in either order (boy-girl, girl-boy)? (16)

Common Core Mathematical Practices

When students analyze Jerry's proposed explanation critically in this last extension activity, they **critique the reasoning of others** and, in doing so, must **attend to the precision** of Jerry's explanation.

Extensions

- How many different families are possible if the total number of children is one, two, three, or four? (2, 4, 8, 16)

- How is the question of the number of different combinations of children (above) related to Pascal's triangle? (See *Patterns and Functions* [Phillips et al. 1991, pp. 28–31].)

- What is the probability of having at least two boys in a family of six?

- Jerry and Pam have two daughters. They want four children altogether. Jerry thinks that they will probably end up with two boys and two girls. Jerry argues, "The probability of having two boys and two girls is 50 percent because the probability of having a girl or a boy is 50 percent. Besides, the probability of having one girl and one boy in a family with two children is 1/2." Pam disagrees and thinks that they will probably end up with three girls and one boy. Who is correct? Why? (The two children that Jerry and Pam have are past events and already determined. To figure the probability of *future* events, they must only consider the *future* unborn children. Therefore, Pam is correct.)

Problem 6: Montana Red Dog

(Adapted from *Dealing with Data and Chance*, illustration 11, pp. 41–45, by Arthur Hyde [Zawojewski et al. 1991], and from Hyde [2006])

Montana Red Dog is a card game that originated in the Old West. It uses a standard deck of fifty-two cards having the four suits (diamonds, clubs, hearts, and spades); the ace is "high," and the jokers are removed. The teacher is the dealer and plays against the class as a whole. The class is arranged into ten groups of two to three students each. The dealer gives each group four cards, leaving twelve cards for the dealer. The dealer turns over the top card of the twelve held, and each group tries to beat the dealer. A group wins if one of its four cards is higher in number than the dealer's card, but it must be of the same suit. At the end of the game, the number of times the groups win is compared with the number of times the dealer wins. The problem: is this game fair?

Note about Montana Red Dog

The game is not fair, because it favors the dealer. Although this problem exposes students exclusively to an empirical analysis of the game, a theoretical analysis, which is beyond the scope of this activity, reveals that the dealer will win about 62 percent of the time.

Materials

☑ Overhead transparency and copies of blackline master 3.5

☑ Oversized deck of playing cards

Teacher's Notes

This problem will develop students' understanding of "fair games" on the basis of a combination of probability and statistics. It will introduce systematic empirical analysis, which will start students on the journey into the process of theoretical analysis in later grades.

In playing the game, groups may look at their own cards but not at other groups' cards. The dealer (i.e., teacher) must not show his or her cards to the class. Each group gets a turn at trying to beat a different card from the dealer's pile.

Play a practice game with the students. First, put a two-column table on the chalkboard with headings "Dealer Wins" and "Dealer Loses," such as the one shown below. The dealer shows the class the top card of the twelve that he or she holds and asks, "Can you beat this?" Then the dealer says, "If you can beat it, show me *one* card from your hand that can beat me; hold it up." (For example, if the dealer holds up a ten of diamonds, the only cards that any group can hold up that will beat the dealer are the jack, queen, and king of diamonds.) The dealer counts the number of groups with a winning card displayed and enters that number under the Dealer Loses column. Because ten groups are playing against the dealer, the number of groups who have beaten the dealer is subtracted from 10 to calculate the number of groups that did not beat the dealer. The difference is entered under the Dealer Wins column. Repeat this process with the subsequent rounds, the dealer holding up the top card in his or her hand and the groups holding up their cards that beat the dealer's. For each round, keep track of the win-loss data by recording them in the table. Once the dealer goes through all twelve cards, a typical two-column table of data might look like this:

Dealer Wins	Dealer Loses
10	0
7	3
7	3
9	1
6	4
6	4
4	6
8	2
6	4
6	4
9	1
8	2
86	34

After examining the data, ask the class, "Do you think this game is fair? Why or why not?" Students' responses may reflect nonprobabilistic reasoning: "It *is* fair, because it is just dumb luck what cards you get." "It is *not* fair because the dealer is holding twelve cards and we hold only four!" "It *is* fair because you shuffled and everybody got random cards." "We will win more because we have four cards against your one card." If such responses emerge, the teacher should ask, "What does it mean to be fair?" Most middle school students will say that a game is fair if the students win half the time, or if the students and the dealer each have an equally likely chance of winning. Then the teacher can ask, "What would fair data in this table look like?" (The totals should be about the same for the "Dealer Wins" and the "Dealer Loses" columns.)

Play two or three more games, shuffling the deck of cards and dealing new hands to the groups and the dealer each time. Again, using a two-column table, gather data from each round, and sum the Dealer Wins and Dealer Loses data after each game is complete. Convert the raw number total for each game into a percent, and have students look for patterns in the data over each game. (The data are likely to indicate a strong advantage to the dealer.) Then pose some hypothetical questions to the students.

- What if the dealer won 90 percent of the time on every game, week after week?

  — Some students may continue to give nonprobabilistic responses, such as, "The dealer is cheating!" If so, ask, "What if the dealer is definitely *not* cheating?"

  — Some students may say, "He had a lucky streak." In response, ask, "What if this 90-percent winning streak lasted all year long, playing the game every day?"

  The goal is to have students question whether something inherent in the Montana Red Dog game makes it more likely for the dealer to win, thus setting up the need to analyze a hand.

Deal the cards for another game. Ask students to examine their hands and to respond to the question, "Who has a good hand now? Show us your cards." Once group members say they believe they have a good hand, ask them to share their four cards with the class and describe what they think makes it a good hand. Many students will immediately indicate that the possession of high cards makes it a good hand. Ask, "What if I turned up a two of clubs, who could beat me?" Typically, six of the ten groups could, to which you can respond, "Do you mean that four of the ten groups cannot even beat the smallest club?" This question helps students realize that no matter how high the cards in their hand, if they do not have a suit that matches the dealer's, they cannot win. Thus, they may begin to develop an early, primitive notion that a good hand has high cards in all four suits.

A common misconception at this point is that students begin to focus on individual hands or trials and not on the long run. The following activity can help move them to thinking more over the long run. Demonstrate how to use blackline master 3.5 by writing on the chalkboard the four cards that a fictional group of four students has: ace of spades, five of spades, six of hearts, and queen of diamonds. Circle each of those cards on the overhead transparency of blackline master 3.5. For the spades column, figure out with the students what cards this hand can beat in spades. (The ace of spades and five of spades together can beat eleven cards: the king, queen, jack, ten, nine, eight, seven, six, four, three, and two of spades.) Write the "can beat" number of 11 at the bottom of the spades column. Then ask, "What cards in the column cannot be beaten by this hand?" There are none, so write the cannot-beat number of 0 at the bottom of the column. For the hearts column, given the hand has a six of hearts, the hand can beat the five, four, three, and two of hearts. The can-beat and cannot-beat numbers written at the bottom of the column are, for hearts, 4 and 8 (seven, eight, nine, ten, jack, queen, king, and ace of hearts), for clubs, 0 and 13; and for diamonds, 10 and 2. Ask, "What is the total of the can-beat numbers?" (25) "What is the total of the cannot-beat numbers?" (23) This outcome means that of the forty-eight cards that the fictitious group cannot see, they can beat twenty-five of the cards.

Distribute a copy of blackline master 3.5 to each student. Have students circle the four cards that they hold in their hand and calculate the can-beat and cannot-beat numbers for their own hands. The notion of the can-beat number feels empirical and powerful—the more high cards, the better the hand. However, have students consider a hand that has the aces and kings of both spades and hearts: this combination certainly *cannot* beat half the cards in the deck. Further, because the four highest cards of the spades and hearts are not in the dealer's hand to be beaten, the can-beat number for spades and hearts is only 11 each. This apparently great hand can beat only twenty-two cards out of the forty-eight not held in the hand. Encountering this dilemma sets up the need to calculate the probability for winning the game.

If a group's can-beat and cannot-beat numbers are both 24, the group can beat 24/48, or half, of the remaining cards. Thus, this group's probability of winning is 0.5. At this point, have all groups calculate their own "can beat/total cards remaining" ratio, figure the probability as a decimal, and write their probability on the chalkboard. On examining the probabilities for this round of hands (you may need to repeat this process for other rounds of hands), students will inevitably be stunned at the low probabilities of winning for most hands. This realization prompts students to wonder what causes the hands' probabilities of winning to be relatively low.

Ask group members to raise their hand if their cards cover all four suits. Of the ten groups, only a few will have a hand that covers all four suits. Ask students to talk about this outcome. Eventually, students say things like, "The dealer doesn't have to worry about suits!" "The dealer determines the suit! He's got it, and you'd better have that same one!" Although analyzing the game's theoretical probabilities is too difficult for middle grades students, the intuitions they develop for analysis based on empirical data help build a conceptual understanding of probabilistic analysis that they can tap in later courses.

Extensions

Have student groups modify the game's rules to make the game fair.

REFERENCES

Hyde, Arthur. *Comprehending Math: Adapting Reading Strategies to Teach Mathematics, K–6.* Portsmouth, N.H.: Heinemann, 2006.

Lappan, Glenda, and Mary J. Winter. "Probability Simulation in Middle School." *Mathematics Teacher* 73 (September 1980): 446–49.

Phillips, Elizabeth, Glenda Lappan, Mary Jean Winter, and William Fitzgerald. *Probability.* Middle Grades Mathematics Project. Menlo Park, Calif.: Addison-Wesley Publishing Co., 1986.

Phillips, Elizabeth, with Theodore Gardella, Constance Kelly, and Jacqueline Stewart. *Patterns and Functions. Curriculum and Evaluation Standards for School Mathematics* Addenda Series, Grades 5–8. Reston, Va.: National Council of Teachers of Mathematics, 1991.

Travers, Kenneth J., and Kenneth G. Gray. "The Monte Carlo Method: A Fresh Approach to Teaching Probabilistic Concepts." *Mathematics Teacher* 74 (May 1981): 327–34.

Watkins, Ann E. "Monte Carlo Simulation: Probability the Easy Way." In *Teaching Statistics and Probability,* 1981 Yearbook of the National Council of Teachers of Mathematics (NCTM), edited by Albert P. Shulte, pp. 210–19. Reston, Va.: NCTM, 1981.

Zawojewski, Judith S., with Gary Brooks, Lynn Dinkelkamp, Eunice D. Goldberg, Howard Goldberg, Arthur Hyde, Tess Jackson, Marsha Landau, Hope Martin, Jeri Nowakowski, Sandy Paull, Albert P. Shulte, Philip Wagreich, and Barbara Wilmot. *Dealing with Data and Chance. Curriculum and Evaluation Standards for School Mathematics* Addenda Series, Grades 5–8. Reston, Va.: National Council of Teachers of Mathematics, 1991.

Patterns and Functions

THE **PROBLEMS** in this chapter aim explicitly at encouraging students to look for patterns in data, tables, and graphs and make generalizations, first in words and then in symbols. As students look for patterns among quantities in the problems and seek ways to represent those relationships, they encounter variables naturally as a way to make sense of problem situations. If we encourage students to generalize—first in words, tables, and graphs and then in symbols—the symbols become more than just symbols: they represent the reasoning and patterns that the students used in solving the problem. Writing algebraic expressions to represent relationships, judging the equivalence of algebraic expressions, and judging equivalence among tables, graphs, and algebraic expressions all provide a solid basis for studying algebra.

Problems 1–6 in this chapter begin with explorations of some important relationships found in beginning algebra courses—linear, quadratic, cubic, and exponential functions. Problems 7–9 explore important features of functions more generally.

You can use each problem with students with various levels of algebraic experience. For example, for beginning algebra students, an appropriate approach might be to generalize the relationships embedded in the problem in words, tables, and graphs, and then move to simple symbolic statements if students are developmentally ready. Problems that require more complicated symbolic statements are appropriate for students who have a bit more experience with symbolic manipulation. Students can solve many such problems using tables or graphs to represent and reason about the relationships. The Teacher's Notes that accompany a given problem discuss the specific mathematics embedded in that problem.

Problem 1: The Race—Linear Functions

(Adapted from *Patterns and Functions,* investigation 1, pp. 55–57 [Phillips et al. 1991])

Pat and his older sister, Terri, run a race. Pat runs at an average of 3 meters every second, and Terri runs at an average of 5 meters every second. In a 100-meter race, Pat gets a 40-meter head start because he runs at a slower pace. Who wins the race? Explain your reasoning.

Teacher's Notes

This problem can introduce linear functions and, in particular, the use of tables, graphs, and symbols to represent and communicate a linear relationship's salient features.

Solution to Problem 1

The race ends in a tie.

See the discussion in the Teacher's Notes for examples of students' strategies.

Some students may use a table as shown in figure 4.1.

Time (seconds)	Distance (meters)	
	Terri	Pat
Start	0	40
1	5	43
2	10	46
3	15	49
?		
10	50	70
?		
20	100	100
t	$5t$	$40 + 3t$

Fig. 4.1. Distances for Terri and Pat

Common Core Mathematical Practices

When students choose various ways to represent their reasoning about the problem numerically, with graphs, tables, or equations, they learn to **use appropriate tools strategically.**

Let groups of students share their solutions. Some may just use an arithmetic argument to figure the time each person takes to reach 100 meters. For example, if Terri runs 5 meters per second, then it will take her 100 meters divided by 5 meters per second, or 20 seconds, to run the race. A similar argument for Pat shows that he also takes 20 seconds to run the race. In this example, each person takes 20 seconds to reach the finish line, so the race ends in a tie. Some students may look at the distance between the two racers. For example, at the start, they are 40 meters apart. After one second they are 38 meters apart; after two seconds 36 meters; and so on. At 20 seconds, they are 0 meters apart. A few students may use a table as shown in figure 4.1. Some students may use equations if they have had some previous experience with algebra.

Extensions

Ask more questions about the race, such as the following:

- Who wins the race if it is 150 meters? By how many meters?

- How long has each person been running when Pat reaches the 75-meter mark?

Use the students' table or create one (fig. 4.1) with the class to open up the discussion and highlight important mathematical aspects of linear functions. Start by asking the following questions:

- What patterns do you observe in the table?

- What are the variables?

- What is the relationship between the two variables?

- What do these relationships look like on a graph? In an equation?

Students may have several observations. As the time increases by 1 second, Terri's distance increases by 5 meters and Pat's distance by 3 meters. To determine Pat's distance, students can also successively add 3 meters to the previous entry for Pat's distance. The constant rate of change between the two variables identifies this relationship as a *linear function*. As the independent variable (x, or t in this example) increases by a constant amount, the dependent variable (y, or D in this example) also changes by a constant amount.

Students should know that distance equals rate times time and be able to write those patterns in symbols. If t represents time in seconds, D_T represents the distance Terri runs after t seconds, and D_P represents the distance that Pat runs after t seconds, then $D_T = 5t$ and $D_P = 40 + 3t$. The running rate for each person is the coefficient of t in the equation. The 40-meter head start is the constant term in the equation that represents Pat's relationship. It is called the y-intercept on that linear function's graph—the place where the graph of the equation $D_P = 40 + 3t$ intersects the y-axis. The y-intercept for the equation $D_T = 5t$ is 0. This equation's graph intersects both axes at 0 (fig. 4.2). In general, one can represent a linear function by the equation $y = b + mx$, where b is the function's y-intercept and m is its slope.

Answering the question about how a graph represents the linear relationship, students might respond that the graph would be a straight line. This question presents a good opportunity to connect the related patterns of change that the students have expressed in words or observed in a table or symbolic statement. For example, pick two successive entries in the table (e.g., $t = 1$ and $t = 2$) and use them to find the corresponding two points on the graph. As time goes from 1 to 2, distance goes from 5 to 10 for the data representing Terri's relationship. These two entries in the table correspond to the points (1, 5) and (2, 10) on the graph for Terri's relationship. On the graph, the horizontal distance between these two points is 1 and the vertical distance is 5. The ratio, $^5/_1$, of these two distances is called the *slope*. The ratio is the same for any two points on the line or corresponding entries in the table. The slope is also the coefficient of the x in the general equation for a linear function, $y = mx + b$. The graph in figure 4.3 illustrates

Common Core Mathematical Practices
When students observe particular patterns of change between two variables embedded in the problem, they learn to *reason abstractly and quantitatively,* and *look for and make sense of structure.*

this relationship by the two points (0, 0) and (10, 50) and the two points (20, 100) and (35, 175).

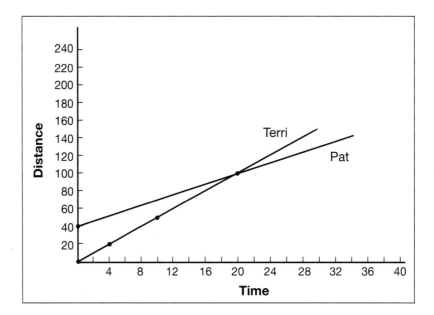

Fig. 4.2. Results of the race between Terri and Pat

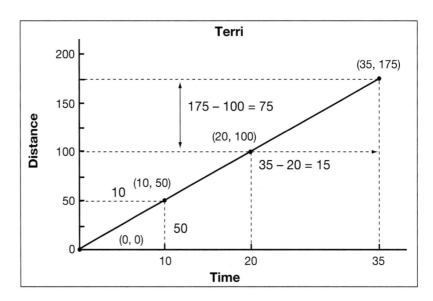

Fig. 4.3. The slope of the line that represents the relationship for Terri's race

Notice that for the points (0, 0) and (10, 50), the slope is the ratio

$$\frac{\text{vertical distance}}{\text{horizontal distance}} = \frac{50}{10} = \frac{5}{1}.$$

For the points (20, 100) and (35, 175), the slope is the ratio

$$\frac{\text{vertical distance}}{\text{horizontal distance}} = \frac{75}{15} = \frac{5}{1}.$$

Several of this chapter's following problems will revisit linear functions.

Problem 2: Rumors—Exponential Functions

(Adapted from *Patterns and Functions,* investigation 1, pp. 6–8 [Phillips et al. 1991])

In Bugsville, USA, Tara, a student at Swat Middle School, decides to start a rumor that the town of Bugsville will declare September 14 as National Bug Day and will close all the schools for the day. She tells two students the rumor with the instructions that each of those students is to repeat the rumor to two more students the next day and that each of those students will tell two more students on the third day, and so on.

- How many students will know the rumor on day 10?

- If Tara starts her rumor on September 1 and 8000 students attend school in the district, will all the students hear the rumor before September 14? Explain your reasoning.

Teacher's Notes

You can use this problem to introduce students to exponential relationships and how to represent the growth pattern associated with those relationships in tables, graphs, and symbols.

Before students explore the problem, be sure that they understand how the rumors will spread. For example, at the start of the first day (or day 0), 1 student, Tara, knows the rumor. At the end of the first day, 2 more students know the rumor for a total of 3. At the end of the second day, 4 more students know the rumor for a total of 7. At the end of the third day, 8 more students know the rumor for a total of 15, and so on. At this point, ask the class if they think that all the students will hear the rumor before September 14. Many students will conjecture that not all the students in the district will hear the rumor before September 14.

Students may propose a variety of ways to find the answer. As you discuss the answers, look for one that used a table, like in figure 4.4, or generate that table with the class. As you generate the table, ask students to predict the next entry. Stop the pattern on day 14. Once you have generated the table, you can promote algebraic understanding by asking many interesting questions about the patterns in the table:

- On what day will approximately half the student population hear the rumor?

Common Core Mathematical Practices
When students explain their reasoning about whether all the students will hear the rumor before September 14, they learn to *make sense of problems and persevere in solving them* and to *construct viable arguments and critique the reasoning of others.*

See the Teacher's Notes for a discussion of student-devised strategies. Some students may use a table to guide their reasoning (see fig. 4.4).

Day	The Number of New People Who Hear the Rumor on a Given Day	Total Number of People Who Have Heard the Rumor on a Given Day, Including Tara
Start of 1st day or Day 0	1	1
1	2	3
2	4	7
3	8	15
4	16	31
5	32	63
6	64	127
7	128	255
?	?	?
10	1024	2047
11	2048	4095
12	4096	8191
13	8192	16383
N	2^n	$2^{n+1} - 1$

Fig. 4.4. An analysis of the rumor problem

- If the rumors continued, on what day would 65,536 students hear the rumor?

- On what day would a total of 524,287 students hear the rumor?

- What two quantities (variables) are changing? Describe the pattern of change between the two quantities.

As the number of the day increases by 1, the number of new people who hear the rumor doubles or increases by a factor of 2. This relationship is called an *exponential relationship*. In the second relationship, the total number of rumors on any given day, as the day's number increases by 1, the total number of rumors more than doubles. It does not increase by a constant factor. The second relationship, therefore, is not an exponential relationship. If students are ready, encourage them to write the relationships in symbols. If n is the number of the day and R is the number of new rumors for that day, then $R = 2^n$. If T is the total number of rumors on any given day, then $T = 2^{n+1} - 1$.

- Graph the pattern represented by $R = 2^n$ (see fig. 4.5). How many rumors have been told on day 10?

- On what day will at least 80 new students have heard the rumor?

- How does the pattern of change in the table show up on the graph?

Common Core Mathematical Practices
When students look at the relationship between the two variables in this problem and discuss how tables, graphs, and equations reflect it, they learn to *reason abstractly and quantitatively,* and *look for and make sense of structure.*

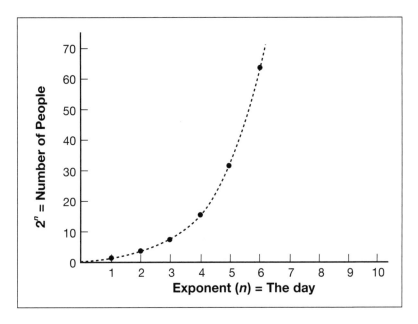

Fig. 4.5. Number of students who hear the rumor on a given day

Illustrating the pattern of change on the graph helps students understand the situation. As n increases by 1 (the horizontal line on the graph), R increases by a factor of 2, or doubles (vertical line). If you draw the vertical lines on the graph, you can easily observe the pattern of change associated with this relationship. The factor 2 is the *growth rate* for this exponential function.

- How does the equation represent the pattern of change, the growth rate?

Students can repeat this problem with different rates. Rumors could triple, quadruple, and so on. In general, any relationship of the form $y = b^n$ where $b > 1$ is an exponential function; b is the growth rate. The graph $y = b^n$ is similar to the graph of $R = 2^n$.

Extensions

- The table in figure 4.6 represents the powers of 2. Observe the pattern in the table. What are the possible values for 2^0 and 2^{-1}?

2^4	16
2^3	8
2^2	4
2^1	2
2^0	?
2^{-1}	?

Fig. 4.6. Investigating the pattern in the powers of 2

- Observe the pattern in the last column in the rumors table (fig. 4.4.) (The numbers are the sum of the first n powers of 2; see fig. 4.7.) What is the number in the fifteenth row? In what row is the total number 32,768? What is the first row in which the sum will exceed 1,000,000?

Row 0	1 = 1
Row 1	1 + 2 = 3
Row 2	1 + 2 + 4 = 7
Row 3	1 + 2 + 4 + 8 = 15
Row 4	?
Row 5	?

Fig. 4.7. Patterns in the last column of the rumors table

Problem 3: Folding Paper—Exponential Functions

(Adapted from *Patterns and Functions*, investigation 3, pp. 14–15 [Phillips et al. 1991])

Fold a sheet of paper in half to create new regions. Have students continue repeatedly folding the paper in half, and ask the following questions:

- How many regions have you created after three folds? After five folds? After 10 folds?

- How many folds will you need to create 128 new regions?

- If the area of the paper is 1 square unit, what is the area of each new region?

Record your answers to the previous questions in a table. Look for patterns in the table.

Materials

☑ 8.5-by-11-inch sheet of paper

Solution to Problem 3

Number of Folds	Number of Regions	Area of the Smallest Region
0	1	1
1	2	1/2
2	4	1/4
3	8	1/8
?		
5	32	1/32
6		
7	128	1/128
?		
10	1024	1/1024
?	?	?
n	2^n	$1/(2^n)$

As the number of folds increases by 1, the number of regions increases by a factor of 2. As the number of folds increases, the area of the smallest regions decreases by a factor of $\frac{1}{2}$. Each of these relationships is an exponential function. The first one is an exponential growth, and the second one is an exponential decay.

Teacher's Notes

This problem presents an opportunity to explore two exponential patterns—an exponential growth and an exponential decay.

Some students may find that tearing the paper or regions in half each time is easier than folding. Discuss the students' strategies for finding the answers. Since the pattern doubles, some students may double the answer for the regions created after five folds to get the number of regions after 10 folds. A table and graph will help focus students' attention on the patterns in this relationship.

- Describe the pattern of change between the number of folds and the number of regions created.

- How does a graph or equation of the relationship represent this pattern of change? (See fig. 4.8.)

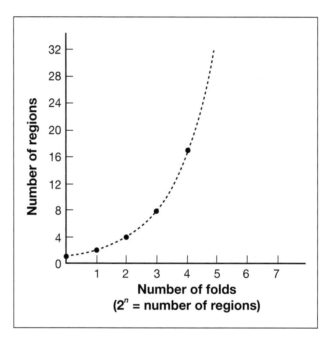

Fig. 4.8. A graph of the pattern of change between the number of folds and the number of regions created

- Compare this pattern with relationships that you have studied previously.

- Describe the pattern of change between the number of folds and the area of the smallest regions created.

- How does a graph or equation of the relationship represent this pattern of change? (See fig. 4.9.)

- Compare this pattern with relationships that you might have studied previously.

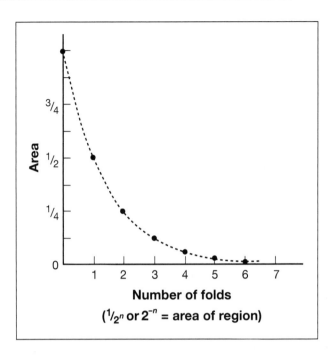

Fig. 4.9. The pattern of change between the number of folds and the area of the smallest regions created

If your class has done the previous problem in this chapter, the students may quickly realize that the pattern of numbers of new regions created after each fold is exactly like the pattern of rumors. If R is the number of regions and n is the number of folds, then $R = 2^n$. The graphs are equivalent.

However, the pattern for the area is a bit different. It is similar to that for the number of regions, but it decreases, not increases. That is, as the number of folds increases by 1, the area decreases by a factor of $\frac{1}{2}$. If A is the area of the smallest region and n is the number of folds, then

$$A = \frac{1}{2^n} \text{ or } A = 2^{-n}.$$

This function is exponential, but because it is decreasing, we call it an *exponential decay pattern*, whereas we call the pattern $R = 2^n$ an *exponential growth pattern*. Be sure to discuss the similarities and differences in the graphs. Students should look again at the horizontal and vertical lines that correspond to entries in the table. End the discussion by having students use a table, graph, or equation to answer the following questions:

- What is the number of regions created after 12 folds?

- If the pattern continues, what is the area of the smallest region?

- What is the number of folds needed to have 512 regions?

Students need the experience of exploring specific functions, such as exponential functions, in different situations to understand fully the functions' important features. In this example, as the independent variable changes by a constant amount, the dependent variable changes by a constant factor.

Extension

- Suppose that the area of the sheet of paper is 64 square inches. What is the number of regions and the area of the smallest region after four folds? After six folds? After n folds?

- How do these relationships compare with those you have previously studied?

Problem 4: Miracle Mike—Linear and Exponential Functions

Adapted from *Patterns and Functions,* investigation 4, pp. 15–17 [Phillips et al. 1991])

Miracle Mike plays for the California Hoops basketball team. After the Hoops won the NBA championship, the manager offered Miracle Mike a million dollars a year for the next twenty-five years, whereas a new rookie for the same team would receive $1 for the first year, $2 for the second year, $4 for the third year, and so on for the next twenty-five years.

- At the end of twenty-five years, who has the greater salary? Who has the greater total salary? Explain your reasoning.

- Are the two salaries the same in any year? Explain your reasoning.

Teacher's Notes

In this problem students compare an exponential growth pattern with a linear growth pattern.

Use a table (see fig. 4.10) to explore the patterns of growth in the exponential and linear functions. Ask the following questions:

- What patterns do you see among the variables? Compare these patterns with ones that you have studied previously.

- Find an equation that represents each pattern. Sketch the graph for each equation.

- Describe how the patterns of change in the table show up in a graph and equation.

- In what year does the rookie's salary overtake Miracle Mike's salary? In what year will the rookie's salary exceed Mike's salary? Explain your answers.

Solution to Problem 4

Many students may use a table like that in figure 4.10 to answer the questions.

Year	Miracle Mike's Yearly Salary	Total Accumulated Salary	Rookie's Yearly Salary	Total Accumulated Salary
1	$1,000,000	$1,000,000	$1	$1
2	1,000,000	2,000,000	2	3
3	1,000,000	3,000,000	4	7
?				
15	1,000,000	15,000,000	2^{14}	32,787
?				
20	1,000,000	20,000,000	2^{19}	1,048,575
?				
25	1,000,000	25,000,000	2^{24}	33,554,431
?				
n	1,000,000	1,000,000n	2^{n-1}	$2^n - 1$

Fig. 4.10. Salaries of Miracle Mike and the rookie

As the number of years increases by 1, Mike's total accumulated salary increases by $1,000,000 each year. That is, the change in the dependent variable (salary) increases by adding a constant each time—in this example, 1,000,000. This growth pattern identifies a linear function. As the number of years increase by 1, Mike's yearly salary does not change. That is, it increases by adding 0 each time. This function is also linear. Its graph is a horizontal line parallel to the x-axis, intercepting the y-axis at 1,000,000. If n is the number of years and T_M is Mike's total salary and Y_M is Mike's yearly salary, then $T_M = 1,000,000n$ and $Y_M = 1,000,000$ (see fig. 4.11).

The second pattern is an exponential function. As the number of years increases by 1, the rookie's yearly salary increases by a constant factor—in this example, a factor of 2. If n is the number of years, T_R is the rookie's total salary, and Y_R is the rookie's yearly salary, then $T_R = 2^n - 1$ and $Y_R = 2^{n-1}$ (see fig. 4.11).

The graph of a linear function is a straight line (fig. 4.11). The constant growth pattern is shown in the graph by the slope of the line. As n increases by 1, represented by the horizontal axis on the graph, Mike's accumulated yearly salary increases by 1,000,000 t, represented by the vertical axis on the graph. The ratio of the change in consecutive years to the change in corresponding yearly salaries is 1,000,000, or the slope of the line. The slope is the coefficient of n in the equations $T_M = 1,000,000n$ and $Y_M = 1,000,000$. T_M is Mike's total accumulated salary and Y_M is Mike's yearly salary in any given year n. In the first equation, the coefficient is 1,000,000, and in the second equation, the coefficient is 0. In general, a linear equation can be represented as $y = b + mx$. The slope or rate of change is m and the y-intercept is b. In the two linear examples in this problem, one has a y-intercept of 0 and the other has a y-intercept of 1,000,000. The graph of the exponential function is the same as the exponential functions discussed in the previous two problems. The y-intercept is 1, and the growth factor is 2.

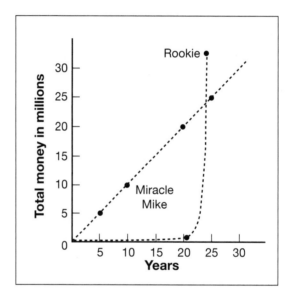

Fig. 4.11. A graphical comparison of salaries

You can find the year when the two yearly salaries are the same by estimating the salary from the table or on the graph. (It is between years 24 and 25.) The algebraic equivalent of this question is "What is the solution to the equation $10^6 n = 2^n - 1$?" *No algebraic algorithm exists to find the intersection point of a linear and an exponential function; the only way is by approximation.*

Although one can ask many questions about this context, this problem's important focus is the comparison between exponential and linear growth patterns.

Extensions

- Use a table and graph to explore the relationships represented by $y = 3^x$, $y = 4^x$, ... $y = b^x$.

- Suppose Mike's yearly salary is \$1 million the first year, \$2 million the second year, \$3 million the third year, \$4 million the fourth year, and so on. What is his accumulated salary for any given year? Use a table and graph to compare this relationship with linear and exponential patterns. (This pattern is not linear or exponential; it is a quadratic pattern.)

Problem 5: Cube Coloring—Linear, Quadratic, and Cubic Functions

(Adapted from *Patterns and Functions,* investigation 4, pp. 17–19 [Phillips et al. 1991])

Suppose we constructed a large cube from 1000 unit cubes. We then painted the large cube's surface and disassembled the large cube into the original unit cubes. How many of the unit cubes have three painted faces, two painted faces, one painted face, and no painted faces? Explain your reasoning.

Hint: Students might simplify the problem by starting with smaller cubes made from 1, 8, 27, ... unit cubes and then look for patterns.

Materials

☑ A large quantity of unit cubes

Solution to Problem 5

If students use a table to record the data for cubes whose side lengths are 1, 2, 3, 4, and more units, interesting patterns should emerge. See the table in figure 4.12.

Dimensions	Number of Unit Cubes Needed	Number of Unit Cubes with Paint on Them			
		Three Faces	Two Faces	One Face	Zero Faces
$2 \times 2 \times 2$	8	8	0	0	0
$3 \times 3 \times 3$	27	8	12	6	1
$4 \times 4 \times 4$	64	8	24	24	8
$5 \times 5 \times 5$	125	8	36	54	27
$n \times n \times n$	n^3	8	$12(n-2)$	$6(n-2)^2$	$(n-2)^3$

Fig. 4.12. Table to organize data from the cube problem

Teacher's Notes

This problem introduces students to two new growth patterns—quadratic and cubic functions. It also promotes students' spatial skills as they move from smaller unit cubes to larger ones, looking for repeating patterns that will help them generalize the new relationships.

If students are having difficulty with the large cube, encourage them to build smaller cubes and look for patterns. Some students may draw the faces on square grid paper, whereas others may build the frame of the cube. After students have had a chance to discuss their strategies, suggest that they organize their data in a table (see fig. 4.12); or, if a group of students has used a table, then use that table. Let the class discuss the patterns they find in the table. The following patterns should emerge:

- The unit cubes with three faces painted are always the eight corners of the original cube (see fig. 4.13).

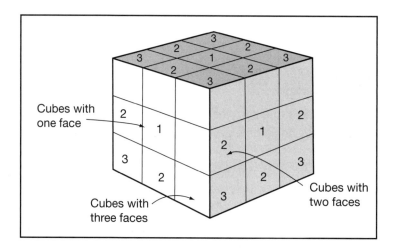

Fig. 4.13. Using a 3 × 3 × 3 cube to simplify the painted-cube problem

- The unit cubes with two faces painted occur on the edges between two corners of the original cube. The number of cubes on each edge is two less than the dimension of the original cube. Therefore, there are $12(n - 2)$ cubes with two faces painted. The numbers in this column have a factor of 12 because these cubes lie on the twelve edges of the original cube.

- The unit cubes with one face painted occur as squares on the faces of the original cube whose dimensions are two less than those of the original cube. The numbers in the one-face column have a factor of 6—each is 6 times a square number—because these cubes lie on one of the six faces of the original cube. There are $6(n - 2)^2$ cubes with one face painted.

- The unit cubes with zero faces painted are a smaller cube in the center of the original cube whose dimensions are two less than the original cube. There are $(n - 2)^3$ cubes with no painted faces.

- The numbers in the three-faces and zero-faces columns are cubic numbers.

Some questions that you can ask are these:

- What are the dimensions of the cube that has 1331 unit cubes with no faces painted?

- What are the dimensions of a cube that has 5046 unit cubes with one face painted? Explain why.

- Could the number 708 occur in the column with two faces painted? Could the number 1000 appear in this column? Explain why.

- How do you know whether you have accounted for all the unit cubes? Explain your reasoning. (The sum of the cubes with zero faces, one face, two faces, and three faces painted is the total number of cubes, n^3.)

Students may notice the patterns of change in each column. If your students are ready to examine them, the patterns of change are interesting and important ideas in beginning algebra. Ask students these questions:

- What are the variables?

- What are the patterns of change among the variables?

- Write an equation that represents each pattern.

The numbers in the three-faces column are always 8. The change from one entry to the next is 0, which is a characteristic of a linear function. Similarly, the change from one entry to the next in the two-faces column is 12, which also represents a linear function.

The change from one entry to the next in the one-face column changes by +6, +18, +30, ... , which is not a constant change. However, if we take successive differences of these numbers, the change is a constant 12. Patterns of change between two variables that are characterized by a constant second difference are *quadratic functions*.

Similarly, the patterns of change in the zero-faces column have a finite third difference. To see this change pattern, extend the table for a few more cubes. The patterns of change with a finite third difference are *cubic functions*. The last row of the table in figure 4.12 gives the symbolic representation for each of these

Common Core Mathematical Practices
When students find the cubes with a certain number of painted sides, they learn to *make sense of problems and persevere in solving them, model with mathematics,* and *look for and express regularity in repeated reasoning.*

functions. For an important follow-up to this discussion, have students examine the patterns of change that they find when they compare the graphs of these functions (see fig. 4.14).

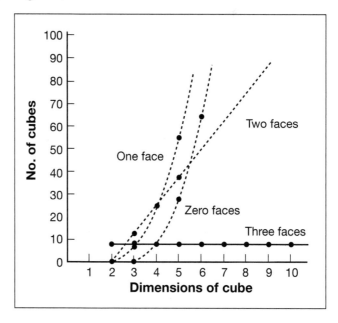

Fig. 4.14. Graphs of numbers of cubes with zero, one, two, and three faces painted

Extensions

Note: The following two extensions would be appropriate to give to students who have some simple algebraic skills in working with linear and quadratic expressions.

- A student observed that the sum of the unit cubes in the three-faces, two-faces, one-face, and zero-faces columns must equal the total number of unit cubes needed to build the original cube and claims that $n^3 = 8 + 12(n - 2) + 6(n - 2)^2 + (n - 2)^3$. Is this statement true? Explain.

- A student observed that the surface area of the cube is equal to the sum of the total number of faces painted and claims that $6n^2 = 8(3) + 12(n - 2)(2) + 6(n - 2)^2(1)$. Is this statement true? Explain.

Problem 6: Maximum Area—Quadratic Functions

(Adapted from *Patterns and Functions*, investigation 1, pp. 41–44 [Phillips et al. 1991])

Tanya Teen started her own summer business—putting on birthday parties for small children. Her neighbors agreed to loan her square card tables to seat the children for refreshments. All the children want to sit together, so Tanya placed the card tables together into rectangles. Only one child could sit on each side of a card table. Her first party had eighteen children.

- How many tables did Tanya need to borrow?
- What are the least and greatest numbers of tables that she needs?

Materials

☑ Square tiles

☑ Grid paper

Solution to Problem 6

Many students will use a table like the one in figure 4.15. The least number of tables needed is 8, and the greatest number is 20.

Length of Rectangle	Width of Rectangle	Perimeter in Units	Area in Units or Total Number of Small Tables
1	8	18	8
2	7	18	14
3	6	18	18
4	5	18	20
5	4	18	20
6	3	18	18
7	2	18	14
8	1	18	8

Fig. 4.15. Rectangles with a perimeter of 18 units

Teacher's Notes

In this problem, students are comparing the relationship among the areas of rectangles (card tables) having a fixed perimeter (number of children who can sit around the rectangle). The problem involves two patterns that students explore. One is the quadratic relationship between the length (or width) and the area of a rectangle having a fixed perimeter. The second pattern is a linear relationship between the length and width of a rectangle having a fixed perimeter. The language of the banquet-tables problem comes from the book *Mouse and Elephant* (Shroyer and Fitzgerald 1986). It is similar to the problem posed in *Curriculum and Evaluation Standards for School Mathematics* (NCTM 1989, p. 103).

You can either use unit tiles to represent card tables or draw the tables on square grid paper. In this example, each card table represents one square unit—its area is one square unit. The number of people at each table represents the perimeter. Place several different arrangements made from unit tiles on the overhead projector screen, and check to be sure that students understand the problem. Only one child can sit on each side of the table—that is, one child for each unit of perimeter. For older students, the problem can be posed as "What is the area of a rectangle with a perimeter of 18 units?" "What is the shape of the rectangle with the greatest area?"

By building tables out of tiles and recording data about possible rectangles in a table, students should be able to observe that a 4-by-5 or 5-by-4 rectangle will seat eighteen children but requires twenty tables. A 1-by-8 or an 8-by-1 by rectangle will seat eighteen children but requires only eight tables. In mathematical language, this observation means that for a fixed perimeter of 18 square units and whole number dimensions, the 1-by-8 rectangle has the least area, whereas the 4-by-5 rectangle has the greatest area. The following questions can further students' understanding of quadratic functions:

- What is the shape of the rectangle with the least area? With the greatest area?

- If the rectangles could have nonwhole-number dimensions, would a rectangle with a greater area be possible? With a smaller area? (If eighteen children attend the party, then the most tables needed is twenty. If the dimensions can be nonwhole numbers, students may say that if a rectangle with greater area exists, its length and width should be between 4 and 5 units. Students will usually try a 4.5-by-4.5 rectangle. Its area is 20.25 square units, which is greater than 20. Trying lengths larger and smaller than 4.5, say 4.4, 4.6, or 4.55, will yield areas that are smaller than 20.25. The shape of the rectangle with the greatest area for a fixed perimeter is a square. In this example it is a 4.5-by-4.5 square with area 20.25 square units and a fixed perimeter of 18. To find a rectangle with a smaller area than 8 square units, students will try smaller and smaller dimensions, such as $\frac{1}{2}$ by 16, $\frac{1}{4}$ by 32 or $\frac{1}{8}$ by 64, …. In each instance, the area gets smaller and smaller. Therefore, no rectangle with the least area exists if the dimensions are real numbers.)

- Suppose that twenty children were coming to the party (i.e., the perimeter of the rectangle is 20), what are the dimensions of the rectangle that has the greatest area? Describe its shape.

- Can you find a pattern that will allow you to predict the rectangle that has the least or greatest area if 24 children come to the party? If *n* children come to the party?

Exploring the area of rectangles having different fixed perimeters may convince students that the rectangle whose shape is a square has the greatest perimeter. For a fixed perimeter of 20 units, the 5-by-5 rectangle has the greatest area. For a fixed perimeter of 24 units, it is a 6-by-6 rectangle. For a fixed perimeter of 34 units, the 8-by-9 rectangle has the greatest area if the dimensions are whole numbers and the 8.5-by-8.5 rectangle has the greatest area if the dimensions are real numbers.

You can push the generalizations in this problem a bit further by asking students to describe some patterns in the table:

- What patterns do you observe in the table? How can those patterns help you predict the dimensions of the rectangle having any fixed perimeter?

- What are the variables? How are those variables related? Describe how those patterns show up in a graph and equation.

- How can you use the graph or equation to predict the dimensions of a rectangle having the greatest area for a fixed perimeter?

One pattern in the table that students may notice is that the length plus the width of a given rectangle is equal to 9, which is half the fixed perimeter, and that the length *times* the width is equal to the area. Ask students why these patterns hold. Students may continue to describe the process in words. To find the rectangle with the greatest area for a fixed perimeter, take half the perimeter and then take half the resulting number, or take one-fourth of the perimeter. This number is the length of the square that has the greatest area for the fixed perimeter. For a perimeter equal to 18, it is $\frac{1}{4} \times 18$, or 4.5; for a perimeter equal to 20, it is $\frac{1}{4} \times 20$, or 5; and so on.

As the length, *l*, increases by 1, the width, *w*, decreases by 1;

$$l = \frac{(18 - 2w)}{2} = 9 - w.$$

This pattern represents a linear pattern whose graph is a straight line with slope equal to −1 and *y*-intercept equal to 9.

Students may also observe in the table that as the length goes from 1 to *n,* where *n* is half the perimeter, the area increases to a certain point and then decreases, and the dimensions then repeat. The increase and decrease increments are the same.

Common Core Mathematical Practices
When students look for patterns and make conjectures about the linear and quantitative relationships in this problem, they learn to *reason abstractly and quantitatively* and *look for and express regularity in repeated reasoning.*

The table has symmetry. If we take successive differences between the areas, we get –6, –4, –2, 0, 2, 4, 6. It we take the differences of the differences (called second difference), we get –2, –2, –2, –2, and –2. The second difference is a constant. As we observed in the previous problem, this pattern represents a quadratic equation.

The linear relationship between the length and width, shown in the graph in figure 4.16, is a line with negative slope—the line decreases as the length increases.

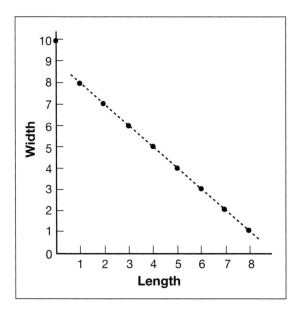

Fig. 4.16. The graph of the length versus the width is linear.

On the area-versus-length graph in figure 4.17, students will observe that as the length increases, the area increases to a maximum point and then decreases. The maximum point on the graph occurs when the length is equal to one-fourth the perimeter. If you draw a vertical line from the maximum point to the x-axis, it divides the graph so that the two halves of the graph are mirror images. We say the graph has symmetry around the maximum point.

To find an equation for the linear pattern for a fixed perimeter of 18 units, students might write $l + w = 9$ or $w = 9 – l$, where l represents the length and w represents the width. For the quadratic equation, if A = area of the rectangle, then $lw = A$. Because $w = 9 – l$, we can substitute the expression for width into the area equation, so that $A = l(9 – l)$. If students have had previous algebraic experience, they may notice that the graph of the area equation—$y = x(9 – x)$, or $y = 9x – x^2$—intercepts the x-axis at $x = 0$ and $x = 9$. These points are called the x-intercepts of the graph. When they substitute these values into the quadratic equation, the resulting area equals zero. Further, students may notice that the point on the graph representing the maximum possible area occurs at a value for x halfway between the x-intercepts, at $x = 4.5$.

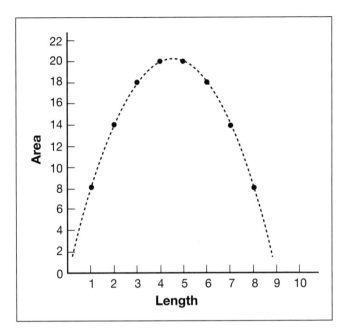

Fig. 4.17. The graph of the area versus the length is a parabola, representing a quadratic function.

More generally, if P is the fixed perimeter, we can write

$$w = \left(\frac{P}{2}\right) - l \ \text{ and } A = l\left(\left(\frac{P}{2}\right) - l \ \right).$$

This problem fosters intuition and understanding for some very important concepts in algebra and calculus. Patterns of rates of change and maximum and minimum points become major focuses in calculus.

Extensions

- Explore the perimeter of rectangles that have a fixed area. Which rectangles have the greatest perimeter? The least perimeter? Start with whole-number dimensions, and extend your work to real numbers. In your work, explore patterns that will help you generalize your findings. Tables, graphs, and equations can be useful for generalizing and representing your patterns. Start with a fixed area of 24 square units.

- Explore other fixed perimeters to help with your generalizations.

The function that describes the relationship between the length, l, and perimeter, P, of a rectangle with fixed area, A, can be represented by the equation

$$P = 2\left(\frac{A}{l} + l\right).$$

Common Core Mathematical Practices
When students explore the situation when the area is fixed and the perimeter can vary, they learn to *look for and express regularity in repeated reasoning.*

Note that if $A = wl$, then $w = A/l$. This is an inverse relationship.

Problem 7: Reading Graphs

(Adapted from *Patterns and Functions*, extension 1.2, pp. 57–60 [Phillips et al. 1991])

The graphs in figures 4.18–4.23 describe different situations. For each graph, name the two variables that are represented and describe the relationship between them. Give as much information as you can. Answer the questions.

1. Jack runs a race (see fig. 4.18).

    •   Explain why the graph is not a straight line.

    •   How fast does Jack run in the first 5 seconds?

    •   How fast does Jack run after 5 seconds?

    •   How long does Jack take to run 50 meters?

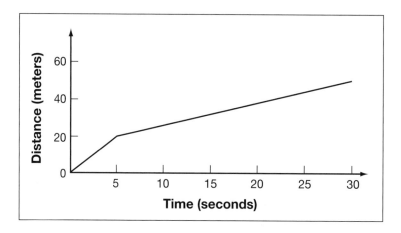

Fig. 4.18. Graph of Jack's race

2. Jack and Jill run a race (see fig. 4.19).

    •   Who wins the race? By how much?

    •   How far from the start did Jill overtake Jack?

    •   How many seconds from the start did Jill overtake Jack?

    •   Who is ahead after 18 seconds? By how much?

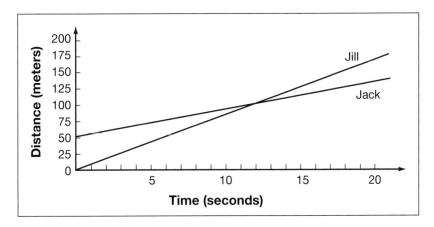

Fig. 4.19. Jack and Jill's race

3. Explore the height from the ground of a rocket launched from a platform (see fig. 4.20).

    •   When time is 0, why isn't the height also 0?

    •   How long does the rocket take to hit the ground?

    •   What is the maximum height of the rocket from the ground?

    •   What is the height after 10 seconds?

    •   At what time does the rocket reach a height of 45 feet?

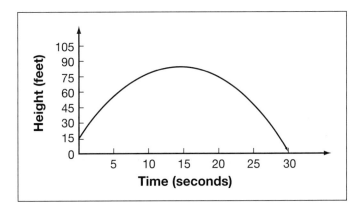

Fig. 4.20. Graph of the height of a rocket versus lapsed time

4. Explore the height of a flag above the ground (see fig. 4.21).

    •   Why does the height vary between 0 and 5 seconds?

    •   Why does the height not vary after 5 seconds?

- Explain the height at 0 seconds.

- How high is the flagpole?

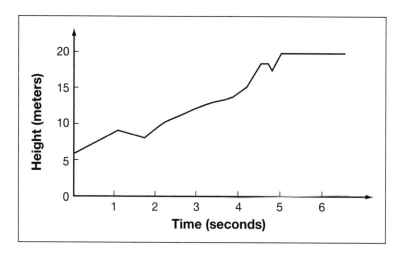

Fig. 4.21. The height of a flag versus lapsed time

5. Investigate Bugsville Booster Club sales (fig. 4.22).

   - Which graph best describes the profit made from the Booster Club sales of Bugsville sweatshirts?

   - Discuss the profit displayed in each graph, and then explain your choice.

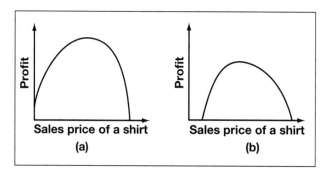

Fig. 4.22. Profit versus sales price of a sweatshirt

6. Describe a cross-country-skiing journey (see fig. 4.23).

   - Describe the skier's journey at points A, B, C, D, E, and F.

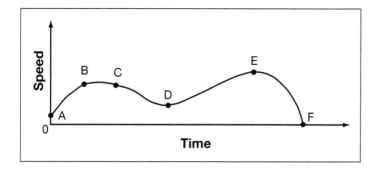

Fig. 4.23. The graph of a cross-country-skier's journey

Solutions to Problem 7

1. The graph is made up of two straight lines; 4 meters/second; $1\frac{1}{3}$ meters per second; ~39 seconds.

2. Jill wins by ~50 meters; ~100 meters; ~12 seconds; Jill is ahead by ~5 meters.

3. The height at time 0 is not 0 because the rocket is being launched from a platform 15 feet off the ground; 30 seconds; ~80 feet; ~75 feet; ~4 seconds and 25 seconds

4. The flag is being raised during the first five seconds, so its height from the ground varies; after 5 seconds it has reached the top of the flagpole so its height does not change; at time 0 the flag is about 5.5 feet off the ground because it is being held by a person who is 5-6 feet tall; 20 meters.

5. Students could provide arguments that support either graph of profit. Graph (a) is not as reasonable, since it shows a profit when zero shirts have been sold. This is unlikely unless the club had a large, up-front donation. Graph (b) is reasonable if we assume the profit was negative for the first few prices, as the club made up their start-up costs.

6. From A to B the skier gradually increases his or her speed. From B to C the skier starts to decrease the speed, which continues to point D. From D to E, the speed gradually increases and then declines sharply from E to F. At F the speed is 0, which means that the skier has stopped or fallen.

Teacher's Notes

In this problem, a graph gives the context for each of several situations. This problem gives students an opportunity to interpret information about the contexts from the graphs, whereas this chapter's previous problems presented contexts verbally. Allow the class to share their interpretations. The answers may vary in some situations.

Extensions

- Make up a story that is represented by a graph. Share your graph with your classmates.

- Make up a story that is represented by a table. Share your table among your classmates for discussion.

- Make up a story that is represented by an equation. Share your equation among your classmates for discussion.

Problem 8: Bottle Functions—an Experiment

(Adapted from *Patterns and Functions,* investigation 2, pp. 60–63 [Phillips et al. 1991])

Investigate the relationship between the volume and the height of a bottle.

- Repeatedly pour a constant amount of liquid into the bottle and record the height of the liquid at the end of each pour.

- Continue this process until the bottle is full.

- Make a graph of the data to study the relationship between the height and the volume of the container.

Materials

☑ Several clear bottles of different shapes

☑ A small measuring cup (1/4 cup)

☑ Graph paper or square grid paper

Suggestions for the Experiment

Give each group a straight-sided, transparent container, different sizes for different groups; some sand, rice, or water; a measuring cup; a ruler; and some graph paper. You may want to try out the size of the measuring cup to be sure that it does not fill up the container too quickly or too slowly. For the first bottle, you may also want to specify the pouring intervals for the axis.

Teacher's Notes

This experiment gives students an opportunity to strengthen their visualization skills in sketching the relationship between the volume and the height of a container. If you use a straight-sided container, the data will approximately lie on a straight line. Some questions that you can ask are these:

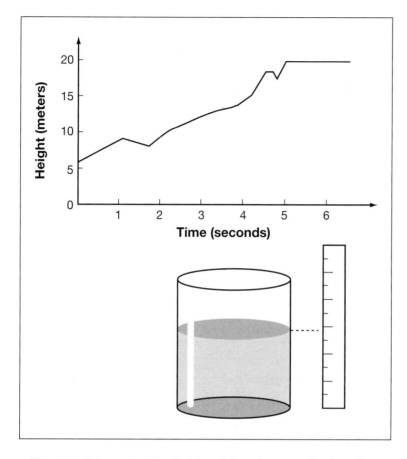

Fig. 4.24. Measuring the height of the contents of a container

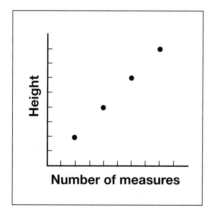

Fig. 4.25. Graphing the height of the contents of a container versus the number of measures added

- What pattern do you notice in the table and graph? (As the height increases by the same amount, the volume increases by a constant amount.)

- Will this pattern continue forever? (It continues until the container overflows.)

- What would the graph look like if we keep on pouring water (sand)? (The height increases up to a limit, but the volume levels off [see fig. 4.26].)

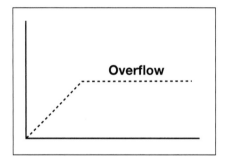

Fig. 4.26. The appearance of the graph after repeated additions

- What is the slope of the line? If we use a container having a different shape, will the graph be a straight line? What would happen if we use a different measure?

As long as the bottles or containers are all straight-sided containers, the graphs will be straight lines. The relationship between the height and volume is a linear function. However, if the bottles are irregularly shaped, then the graphs will not be straight lines. Try some interesting shapes—for example, bottles with a hole in the middle or flasks.

Extensions

- Explore the relationship between the height and volume of containers with irregular shapes, such as those in figures 4.27 and 4.28(b). As the height increases, how does the volume change? How is this pattern of change represented in a table and graph? One such graph appears in figure 4.29(b).

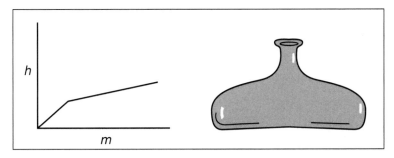

Fig. 4.27. Does the graph represent the height of the contents
of the flask pictured?

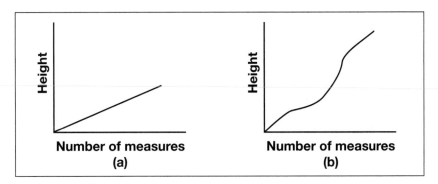

Fig. 4.28. Graphs of the height of the contents of two containers

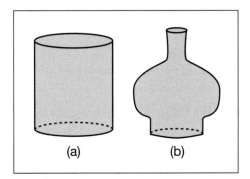

Fig. 4.29. Matching the graphs in figure 4.28 to the corresponding containers

- Explore the rate of change as you draw water off in equal measures
  from the container like the one in figure 4.30. Note: From the chem-
  istry laboratory, borrow a bottle that that allows water to be drawn
  off the bottom. Graph the height of the contents of the bottle as you
  draw successive measures off (see fig. 4.31).

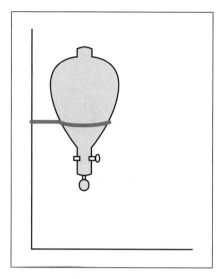

Fig. 4.30. Bottle that allows contents to be drawn off from the bottom

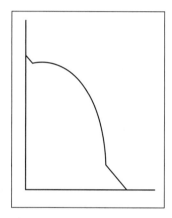

Fig. 4.31. Graph of the height as successive measures are drawn off

Problem 9: The Function Machine

(Adapted from *Patterns and Functions,* investigation 3, pp. 67–70 [Phillips et al. 1991])

Use a function machine to investigate the following:

- Given the input values and a rule, determine the corresponding values of the output values.

- Determine the rule that relates each input value to its corresponding output value in the Function Machine.

Materials

☑ A function machine for the overhead projector (figs. 4.32 and 4.33)

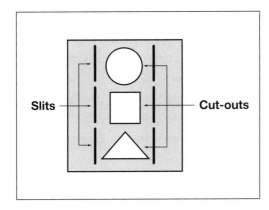

Fig. 4.32. A function machine made from a piece of paper
with cutouts and slits

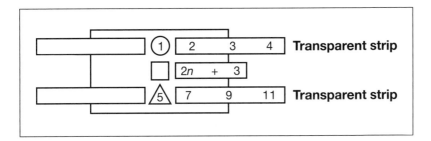

Fig. 4.33. A function machine for the rule 2n + 3

Function Machine

To make a function machine, take a blank sheet of paper and cut out three
holes—one circle, one square, and one triangle—in vertical alignment (see fig.
4.32). On each side of the shapes, make a vertical slit. Make several transparent
strips of paper; the strips should be wide enough to be slipped through the slits.
Record the numbers needed to illustrate a certain function on two of the strips.
On another strip, record the rule (fig. 4.33). Expose two shapes, and let students
determine the appropriate response for the third shape. The circle is called the
input set, and triangle is called the *output* set. The square shape is the associated
rule or function. The values of the input represent the values for the *independent
variable,* and the values for the output represent the values of the *dependent variable.*

Teacher's Notes

This problem approaches functions more formally. A function is a rule that as-
sociates every member in one set with exactly one member in a second set. This
definition has three important parts: the two sets and the rule that relates members in one set with members in the second set.

A function machine is an interesting way to introduce students to the concept of a function. To start the problem, use a specific rule—for example, $2n + 3$—and the corresponding input and output sets of values. Expose one or two pairs of numbers, and ask the class to guess the rule (fig. 4.33). For an easier start, expose the input value and rule and have class predict the output value. Some suggestions for functions appear in figure 4.34. You can also use other rules, such as those studied in previous problems, for example,

$$2n, 2n-1, \frac{n(n+1)}{2}, 2^n, \text{ and } 2^n - 1.$$

Encourage students to make up other rules and try them on their classmates.

Input	1	2	3	4	5		10		x
Output	5	7	9	11			23		2x + 3
The rule is "double the input and add three."									

Input	−2	−1	0	1	2		10		x
Output	−8	−1	0	1	8		1000		x^3
The rule is "each number in the input is paired with its cube."									

Fig. 4.34. Possible functions for the function machine

Algebraic notation writes the first pattern's functional relationship in problem 7 as follows: if x is a member of the first set and y is a member of the second set, then $y = 2x + 3$. The algebraic notation for the second pattern in problem 7 is $y = x^3$. Students can also write these patterns as $f(x) = 2x + 3$ and $f(x) = x^3$. The notation $f(x)$ is read "f of x" or "the function evaluated at x." The input set is called the *domain,* and the output set is called the *range.*

Common Core Mathematical Practices

When students look for patterns and make a conjecture, they learn to **look for and express regularity in repeated reasoning.**

Summary

The problems in this chapter offer examples of how students can explore the mathematical ideas embedded in a problem through a variety of algebraic experiences. Each problem also illustrates the appeal of "mathematics as a science of patterns." Students solving problems will reveal many different patterns, for example, linear, quadratic, cubic, and exponential functions. However, these patterns do not automatically appear in students' discussions or solutions. Teachers need to bring these patterns to the forefront during their investigation summaries. The patterns emerge as students study the relationships between quantities and the way a change in one quantity influences a change in the other. This chapter's problems are not a complete development of these functions; instead, they can serve as introductions to these ideas or as examples that can be used during a comprehensive development of the ideas of functions.

REFERENCES

National Council of Teachers of Mathematics (NCTM). *Curriculum and Evaluation Standards for School Mathematics.* Reston, Va.: NCTM, 1989.

Phillips, Elizabeth, with Theodore Gardella, Constance Kelly, and Jacqueline Stewart. *Patterns and Functions. Curriculum and Evaluation Standards for School Mathematics* Addenda Series, Grades 5–8. Reston, Va.: National Council of Teachers of Mathematics, 1991.

Shroyer, Janet, and William Fitzgerald. *Mouse and Elephant: Measuring Growth.* Middle Grades Mathematics Project. Palo Alto, Calif.: Dale Seymour Publications, 1986.

Appendix

Chapter 2 Blackline Masters

Theses blackline masters are available for download on www.nctm.org/more4u.

Five-by-Five Dot Grids

Blackline Master 2.3
Centimeter Grid Paper

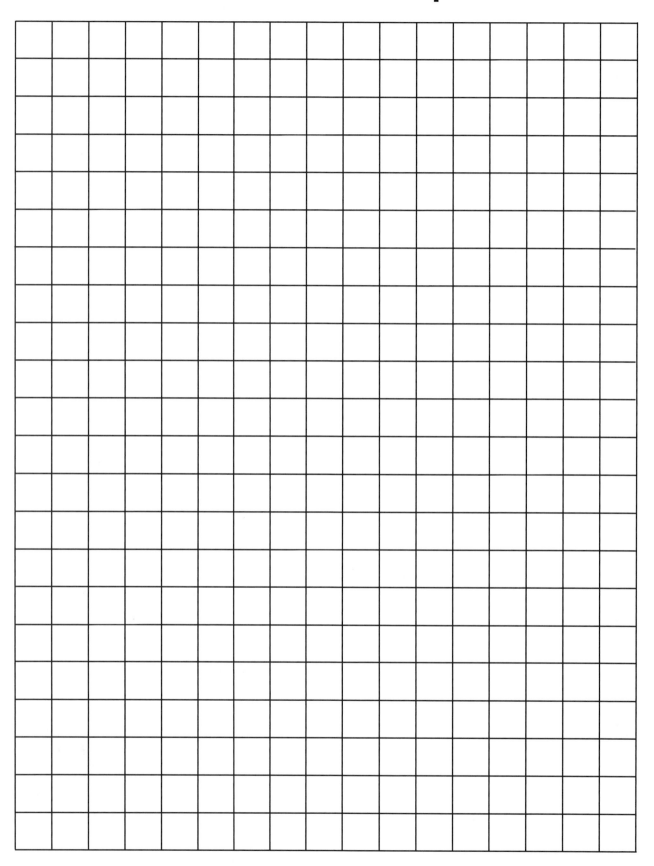

142

Blackline Master 2.4
Isometric Dot Paper

Blackline Master 2.5
Grazing Cows

- A farmer tied his cow, Mooey, to a post with a rope 5 meters long. How many square meters of grazing ground does Mooey have? Explain your method for finding the answer.

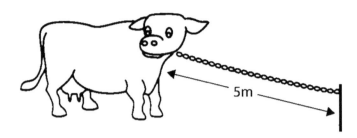

- The farmer moves Mooey to another field and ties her to a post with the same rope at the corner of a closed shed 3m by 3m in the field. How many square meters of grazing ground does Mooey have? Explain your method for finding the area.

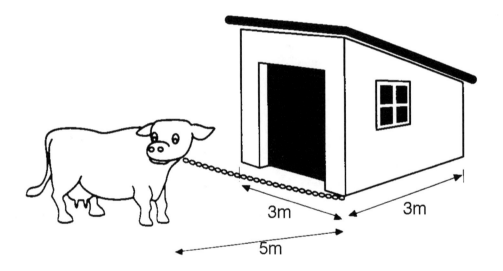

144

The Area of Polygons

1. Find the area of the figures below.

2. The figure below has two holes (shaded regions). Find the area of the figure.

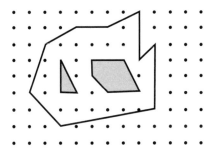

3. On the square-dot paper below, draw a rectangle 3 units by 2 units. Divide the rectangle into two regions that have the same area. Find as many different ways as you can to do so.

Proving the Pythagorean Theorem

For each right triangle, cut out the five pieces of the square of the hypotenuse and reassemble the five pieces so they fill the squares on the two legs of the right triangle. Is this possible? Explain how this process proves that the Pythagorean theorem is true.

Triangle A

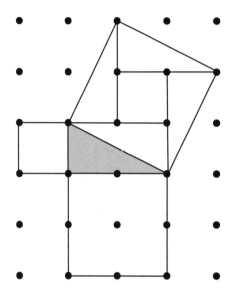

Triangle B

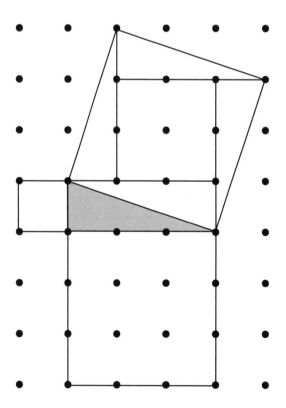

Similar Shapes

- Enlarge figure A by doubling each side to create a similar figure B.

- Enlarge figure A by tripling each side to create a similar figure C.

- Enlarge figure A by quadrupling each side to create a similar figure D.

- Record the perimeter and area of each figure in a table.

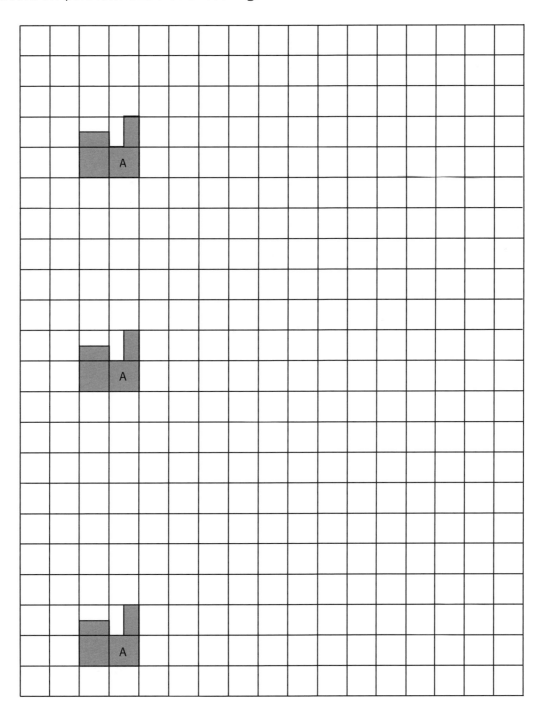

Similar Shapes

Figure	Length of the Base	Perimeter	Area
A	2		
B			
C			
D			

- Look for patterns in the table. What can you say about the relationship between the length of sides, perimeter, and area of two similar figures?

- If you multiply the length of figure A's base by 5, what is the perimeter and area of the new figure?

- If the perimeter of a new similar figure is 64 cm, what is the length of the base of the new figure? What is its area?

- If the area of a new figure is 300 square cm, what is the length of the base of the new figure?

- Compare the corresponding angles of two similar figures.

Building Staircases

- Build a staircase like staircase A (see diagram) using identical cubes.

- Build staircase B so that each dimension is exactly twice as large as the corresponding dimensions of staircase A.

- Build staircase C so that each dimension is exactly three times as large as the corresponding dimensions of staircase A.

- Build staircase D so that each dimension is exactly four times as large as the corresponding dimensions of staircase A.

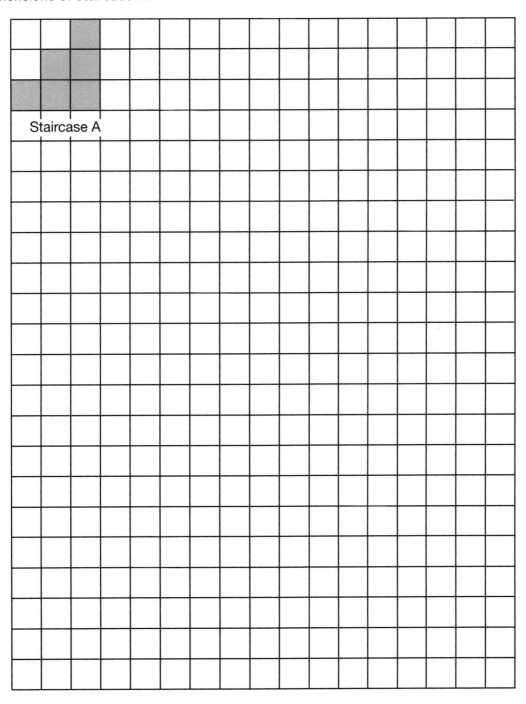

Staircase A

Building Staircases

- Record the height, surface area and volume of each staircase in a table.

Staircase	Height	Surface Area	Volume
A	2 units		
B			
C			
D			

- If the height of staircase A is multiplied by 2, compare the height, surface area, and volume of staircase A with those of staircase B.

- If the height of staircase A is multiplied by 3, compare the height, surface area, and volume of staircase A with those of staircase C.

- If you multiply the height of staircase A by 4, compare the surface area and volume of staircase A with those of resulting staircase D.

- If the volume of a new similar figure is 3000 cubic units, what is the height of the new figure? What is its surface area?

- If the surface area of a new figure is 350 square units, what is the height of the new figure?

Representing Buildings Made from Cubes

- On a building mat, build the building represented in the base plan shown.

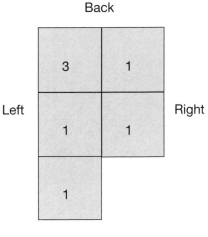

How many cubes do you need to build the bottom layer? How many cubes do you need to build the building?

- Turn the building mat so that you can look at the front, back, left, and right views of the building. Match each view with one of the views below:

I) 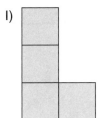 II)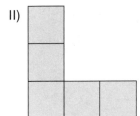

III) 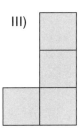 IV)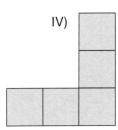

Representing Buildings Made from Cubes

Which view is that from the front side? Back? Right? Left?

- What do you observe about the four views?

- Build the following building on your mat plan:

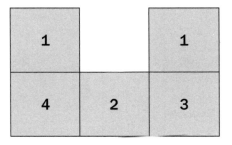

Floor Plan

View the building from the front, back, right, and left sides. Which view of the building does each view represent? Use these views to sketch the other three views.

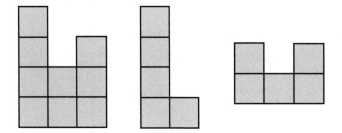

Parallelogram and Triangular Grids

The following grids are formed by sets of parallel lines:

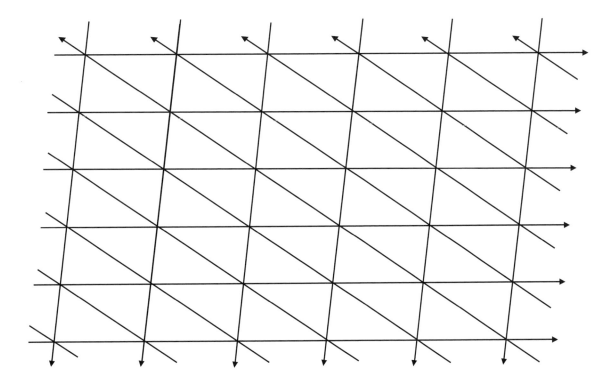

Blackline Master 2.12
Slides, Flips, and Turns

You can move figures about a plane by transformations. The pictures below show figures being transformed by a slide, reflection, and rotation.

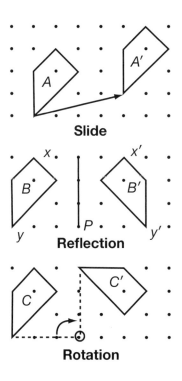

Figure A' is the slide image of figure A. The slide arrow shows the direction of the slide. In this example, by using the dot paper we can say the direction is 4 to the right and 1 up.

Figure B' is the reflection image of figure B about line p. Notice that the reflection line is the perpendicular bisector of a line segment joining a point to its image.

Figure C' is the image of figure C under a rotation around the point O. The rotation or turn is indicated by the size of the angle. The angle has a point as its vertex and sides that connect two corresponding points on the figures with O.

- Which figures are slide images of figure A? Indicate the slide arrow.

  Which figures are reflection images of figure A? Find the flip line.

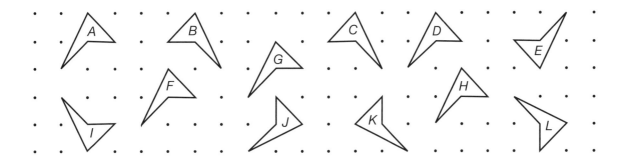

- Draw each reflection image using the dotted line as the reflection line.

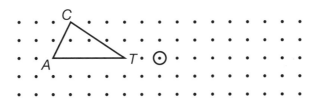

- Rotate figure *CAT* 180 degrees around point *O*. Check your result by using tracing paper (trace figure *CAT*, and turn the tracing paper copy to see if fits on top of your answer).

- Describe one motion that will map the first figure onto the second.

  Map figure *A* onto figure *B*.

  Map figure *A* onto figure *C*.

  Map figure *B* onto figure *D*.

  Map figure *B* onto figure *E*

Map figure *E* onto figure *G*.

Map figure *C* onto figure *E*.

Map figure *A* onto figure *F*.

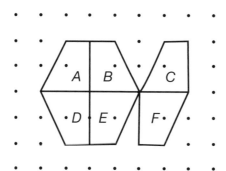

- Examine what occurs if you reflect a figure over two parallel lines. That is, reflect figure *A* over line *c* to form image *A'*, then reflect figure *A'* over line *d* to form image *A''*. How is figure A related to image *A''*? Is it possible to get from figure *A* to image *A''* in one motion? Describe.

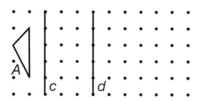 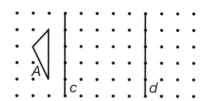

- Repeat the previous problem, but this time do two reflections over intersecting lines.

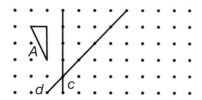 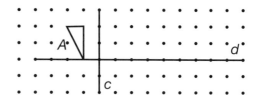

What prediction might you make about the results obtained by doing two reflections over intersecting lines?

Appendix

Chapter 3 Blackline Masters

Theses blackline masters are available for download on www.nctm.org/more4u.

Sum of Seven: A Two-Person Game

Rules of Play

- Decide who is the player and who is the opponent.

- The player and the opponent each start with ten points.

- Each time the player rolls a sum of 7, the opponent must transfer three points to the player.

- Each time the player rolls a sum *other* than 7, the player must transfer one point to the opponent.

- Record the result of each roll on the score sheet (below).

- The participant with the most points at the end of ten rolls is the winner.

- A participant who runs out of points before the end of ten rolls automatically loses.

Score Sheet

	Sum of 7? *Transfer 3 points to the player.* Not a Sum of 7? *Transfer 1 point to the opponent.*									
	Roll Number (10 Rolls per Game)									
	1	2	3	4	5	6	7	8	9	10
Player 10										
Opponent 10										

Sum of Seven Recording Sheet

How many different sums can result from rolling two number cubes, each numbered 1 through 6? Fill in this chart to figure out the answer.

	Die No. 1					
+	**1**	**2**	**3**	**4**	**5**	**6**
1						
2						
3						
4						
5						
6						

Die No. 2

Blackline Master 3.3
A Look at Average Wage

The head of the employees' union in the Millstone Manufacturing and Marketing Company was negotiating with Mr. Millstone, the company's president. The union head said, "The cost of living is going up. Our workers need more money. No one in our union earns more than $36,000 a year."

Mr. Millstone replied, "It's true that costs are going up. It's the same for us—we have to pay higher prices for raw materials, so we get lower profits. Besides, the average salary in our company is over $44,000. I don't see how we can afford a wage increase at this time."

That night the union official conducted the monthly union meeting. A sales clerk spoke up, "We sales clerks make only $20,000 a year. Most workers in this union make $30,000. We want our pay increased to at least that level!"

The union official decided to take a careful look at the salary information. The payroll department gave him a printout of the following salary information from a computer spreadsheet, and he summarized the data in a table like the one below.

Type of Job	No. of Employees	Salary	Union Member?
President	1	$500,000	No
Vice-President	2	$260,000	No
Plant Manager	3	$110,000	No
Foreman	12	$ 36,000	Yes
Workman	30	$ 30,000	Yes
Payroll Clerk	3	$ 27,000	Yes
Secretary	6	$ 24,000	Yes
Sales Clerk	10	$ 20,000	Yes
Custodian	5	$ 16,000	Yes
Total	72	$3,187,000	—

The union head wanted to check what the president said about the average salary, and therefore, calculated the mean as follows:

$$\text{MEAN} = \frac{\$3,187,000}{72} = \text{approximately } \$44,263.89$$

"Hmmmm," the union head thought, "Mr. Millstone is right, but the mean salary is pulled up by those high executive salaries. It doesn't give a really good picture of the typical worker's salary."

From *Reasoning and Sense-Making Activities for Grades 5–8,* edited by Elizabeth Phillips and Judith Zawojewski. Copyright © 2011 by the National Council of Teachers of Mathematics, Inc. www.nctm.org. All rights reserved. May be photocopied for personal use or classroom distribution only. For permission to copy or distribute this material for all other purposes, contact Copyright Clearance Center, www.copyright.com.

A Look at Average Wage

Then the union official thought, "The sales clerk is sort of right. Each of the thirty workmen makes $30,000. That's the *most common* salary—the mode. However, there are thirty-six union members who don't make $30,000—of those, twenty-four make less, whereas only twelve make more.

Finally, the union official said to himself, "I wonder what the *middle* salary is?" He thought of the employees as being lined up in order of salary, low to high. The middle salary (called the *median*) is midway between employee 36 and employee 37, and both employees make $30,000. Thus, the middle, or *median*, salary is $30,000.

Questions

1. If the 24 lowest-salaried workers' salaries were all moved up to $30,000, what would be—

    a. the new median?

    b. the new mode?

    c. the new mean?

2. What salary position do you support, and why?

Light-Bulb Life

Testers randomly selected light bulbs from three companies and tested them for longevity. The testers recorded the number of hours that each of the bulbs burned and made the stem-and-leaf plots below. Examine the data for each company, and use inspection (where no or little calculation is needed) or a scientific calculator (the statistics function) to determine the number of tests, the range of the data, the mean, the median, and the standard deviation. Fill the values in the table below.

Company A

```
2 | 7 9   (This row indicates data points 27 and 29.)
3 | 2 3 9
4 | 5 6
5 | 7 8 9
6 | 1 5 8 9
7 | 3 4 7 9
8 | 3 5 6 7 8 9 9
9 | 2 6 7 8 9
```

Company B

```
5 | 4 7 8
6 | 0 0 0 2 2 4 5 5 5 6 8 8 9
7 | 1 1 2 3 4 5 5 5 6 6 7
8 | 2 9
9 | 1
```

Company C

```
3 | 7
4 | 5
5 | 1 5 8 9 9
6 | 0 1 2 2 3 3 5 5 8
7 | 0 0 2 2
8 | 0 3 4 4 5 6 7 9
9 | 2 3
```

Summary Statistics for Each Company

	No. of Tests	Range	Mean	Median	Standard Deviation
Company A					
Company B					
Company C					

Montana Red Dog Recording Sheet

♠ Spades	♥ Hearts	♦ Diamonds	♣ Clubs
A	A	A	A
K	K	K	K
Q	Q	Q	Q
J	J	J	J
10	10	10	10
9	9	9	9
8	8	8	8
7	7	7	7
6	6	6	6
5	5	5	5
4	4	4	4
3	3	3	3
2	2	2	2

♠ Spades	♥ Hearts	♦ Diamonds	♣ Clubs
A	A	A	A
K	K	K	K
Q	Q	Q	Q
J	J	J	J
10	10	10	10
9	9	9	9
8	8	8	8
7	7	7	7
6	6	6	6
5	5	5	5
4	4	4	4
3	3	3	3
2	2	2	2